# Developing Professional Skills:
# **Criminal Law**

## Douglas A. Blaze

*Art Stolnitz and Elvin E. Overton Distinguished Professor of Law*
*and Director of the Institute for Professional Leadership*
*University of Tennessee College of Law*

## Joy Radice

*Associate Professor of Law*
*University of Tennessee College of Law*

Series Editor: Colleen Medill

**WEST ACADEMIC**
PUBLISHING

© 2017 LEG, Inc. d/b/a West Academic
    444 Cedar Street, Suite 700
    St. Paul, MN 55101
    1-877-888-1330

West, West Academic Publishing, and West Academic are trademarks of West Publishing Corporation, used under license.

Printed in the United States of America
ISBN: 978-0-314-27980-4

# Preface

**LAW SCHOOLS TODAY ARE** increasingly engaged in teaching professional legal skills. The growing emphasis on skills education is partially in response to the criticism that the traditional law school curriculum does not adequately train students to function as lawyers. The high cost of legal education, coupled with a changing legal profession and tight job market for law school graduates, has intensified the demand for greater integration of skills training into the law school curriculum.

Incorporating skills training into doctrinal courses, however, can be challenging. This is particularly true for law school courses taught in the first year. Elaborate simulations can crowd out coverage of fundamental legal concepts and doctrines, frustrating both the professor and the students. The professor may feel that there is never enough time to adequately cover the subject matter. The students feel that there is never enough time, period.

The reality, though, is that including skills training can substantially enhance teaching and learning of doctrine. Carefully crafted skills exercises can significantly increase the students' engagement in the learning process and can significantly increase the students' depth of understanding of the legal doctrine. This can be particularly true in a statutorily focused course like Criminal Law. The use of skills exercises can force students to grapple with statutory language in ways that even the most skilled use of the Socratic Method cannot replicate. And students have an opportunity in writing to apply new facts to the law they are learning before taking the course's final exam.

*Developing Professional Skills: Criminal Law* is designed to provide engaging skills training to law students in a time-efficient way. Each chapter in the book focuses on one of the following core legal skills:

— Client counseling;

— Legal drafting;

— Negotiation; and

— Advocacy.

*Developing Professional Skills: Criminal Law* is intended to make a first-year Criminal Law course fun for the students and the professor. The standard classroom experience of reading cases and answering questions generally is not what students expect when they enter law school. They expected to do what lawyers do more broadly. As attorneys, students will encounter interesting, demanding, and sometimes unreasonable clients. They will deal with constantly evolving technology, as well as financial and time management constraints. But most of all, they will be presented with interesting and challenging problems to solve. Although no book can truly simulate the rich tapestry of legal practice, the skills exercises in this book can offer students a glimpse into practice while significantly enhancing and enriching the students' learning.

Students are expected to spend one or two hours outside of class preparing the skills assignments in each chapter. Professors can choose to use all of the exercises or just a few depending on the structure of the course and the time available. A comprehensive Teacher's Manual contains electronic templates for assignments that can be provided to the students. This allows the students to complete and submit the exercises electronically.

The Teacher's Manual also provides the professor both guidance and discretion in deciding how much time to devote to the exercises. The professor may just generally discuss the exercise and the students' work. Or the professor has the option to expand the discussion to include concepts of professional responsibility, the norms of modern legal practice, and a brief introduction to the skill covered. Suggestions for how to incorporate these into the classroom discussion are included in the Teacher's Manual. The Manual also includes short introductions to the skills of interviewing, counseling, negotiation, and oral argument.

We want to thank Professor Collen Medill at the University of Nebraska College of Law (and previously at the University of Tennessee) for asking us to be part of the Developing Professional Skills series that she developed for West Academic Publishing. We also want to acknowledge how fortunate we are to be part of the faculty at the University of Tennessee College of Law where skills development is valued and a project like this is supported. We are especially grateful to our colleague Professor Paula Schaefer for her guidance, encouragement, and helpful comments. We also want to thank our Criminal Law students who, over the past several years, have worked through various versions of these exercises. Finally, we want to thank Christy Smith and Meagan Willis for their invaluable research assistance.

— Doug Blaze and Joy Radice

# Introduction

*Developing Professional Skills: Criminal Law* introduces you to
skills that differentiate the law student from the experienced legal
practitioner. Like any type of skill, acquiring professional lawyering
skills takes time and patience. Most of all, it takes practice. Each
chapter in this book provides you with the opportunity to practice
a legal skill that you will need and use again and again after you
graduate.

The chapters of this book are organized around the topics that are
usually covered in a substantive Criminal Law course. In Chapter One,
you will be introduced to criminal law, statutory interpretation, and the
skill of oral advocacy. In Chapter Two, you will consider the purposes
of punishment as you negotiate as either the prosecutor or defense
lawyer in a robbery case involving a homeless veteran suffering
from PTSD, alcoholism, and possible drug addiction. Chapter Three
presents you with the difficult policy choices involved in drafting a
statute that focuses on mens rea and levels of culpability.

Chapter Four provides a challenging exercise requiring you to
interview and counsel a client that is treating her sick eight-year-
old daughter solely through faith healing and prayer. In Chapter
Five, you have to draft an email to your boss, the District Attorney,
recommending the appropriate charge in a homicide case arising
out of a road rage incident. Felony murder is the focus of Chapter
Six, which requires you to draft an indictment in a case against a
woman who started a fire in a garbage can that spread and resulted
in two deaths. Chapter Seven gives you the chance to prepare and
make a closing argument on behalf of either the state or one of the
two defendants charged with attempt and conspiracy based on
unsuccessful efforts to rob a convenience store.

In Chapter Eight, you are asked to draft a sentencing memorandum in a high-profile sexting case. In Chapter Nine, the shooting of a suspected intruder in the middle of the night gives rise to second degree murder charges. The exercise requires you to counsel your client regarding a plea offer from the state and, if appropriate, negotiate further regarding the offer. Finally, in Chapter Ten you must advocate and negotiate on behalf of your client in a case involving principles of accomplice liability and criminal responsibility.

Client counseling, legal drafting, advocacy, and negotiation are critical core skills of the legal profession. The exercises in *Developing Professional Skills: Criminal Law* provides you with the opportunity to begin to develop these skills while deepening your understanding of criminal law.

# Table of Contents

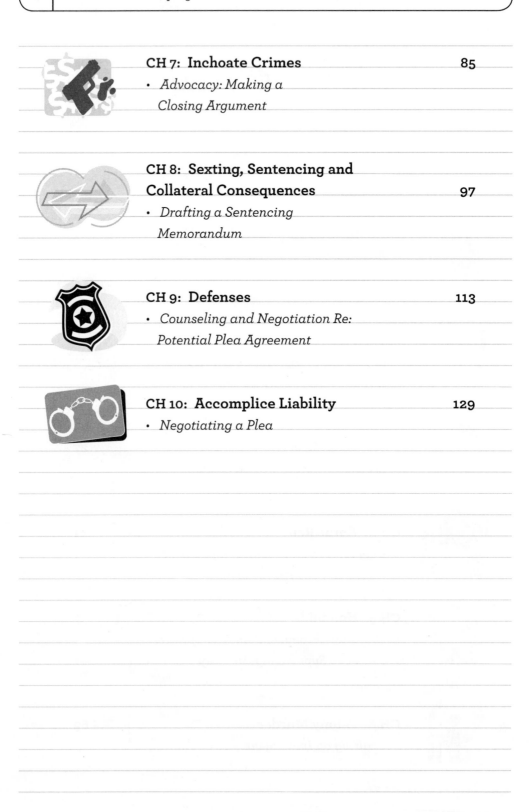

Developing Professional Skills:

# CRIMINAL LAW

# Introduction to Criminal Law
## *Advocacy: An Oral Argument in the Court of Appeals*

**YOUR SUPERVISING ATTORNEY** enters your office and drops a file on our desk. You suspect that he's assigning you your first case. He opens the file and says:

> *You impressed us as a summer law clerk. So I'm assigning you to this new Baxter case. Justin Baxter wants to appeal his conviction for driving under the influence—a DUI. It's a good case to cut your teeth on. And it's an issue of first impression for the Court of Appeals. Apparently, Baxter was convicted after only five hours of jury deliberation, and an article in the News Sentinel described the case as "a slam dunk" for the prosecution. According to witness testimony, which you can read in the file, Baxter was riding a bike home from a law school party at around midnight. You'll see from the charges that Officer Anderson thought Baxter was drunk because Baxter knocked over a garbage can and almost hit a pedestrian on Main Street. Baxter, who is a third-year law student, isn't fighting whether he drank too much that night. He's appealing because he says that our DUI statute doesn't cover riding a bike when you are drunk. The Baxter file goes into more detail. It has the relevant statute, the police warrant, excerpts of testimony from the trial, and a useful Court of Appeals case decided in 2015. So please get ready to argue the case in front of the Court of Appeals. I will let you know the date as soon as the court sets the case on its docket.*

▶ **Applicable Statute**

**§ 39–18–504. Driving Under the Influence.**

1. It is unlawful for any person to be in physical control of any vehicle on a public road, street, or waterway while under the influence of alcohol, marijuana, a narcotic drug, or drug producing stimulating effects on the central nervous system.

2. The crime of driving under the influence is a Class A misdemeanor punishable by a fine of $500, or a period of incarceration not exceeding three days, or both.

▶ **Affidavit of Complaint**

# CRIMINAL COURT
### AFFIDAVIT OF COMPLAINT

*The affiant, <u>Officer Patricia Anderson (Identification No. 2235)</u>, after first being duly sworn according to law, states that a criminal offense has been committed in this county, by the defendant, JUSTIN THOMAS BAXTER, whose last known address is 1057 Main Street.*

Further, the affiant makes oath that the essential facts constituting the said offense and the sources of the affiant's information are as follows:

*The defendant committed the offense of Driving Under the Influence in violation of Section 39–18–504 of the Criminal Code. This incident occurred in front of the Mini Mart Deli at 505 Main Street. The affiant heard a loud crash and saw the defendant getting up from hitting a large city garbage can. The defendant was riding on the sidewalk toward the affiant's police cruiser, which was parked across from the Mini Mart Deli. As the defendant rode toward the affiant, the defendant was traveling downhill, swerving dramatically, and repeatedly ringing a bell on his bike. The defendant struggled to control the bike.*

*The bike was pink and bright green with a basket. The defendant almost hit two employees who were pulling down the front gate of the Mini Mart Deli. They saw him coming and jumped out of the way. The defendant swerved to miss them and hit a light post, falling off his bike again. The affiant left the police cruiser and ran over to the defendant. As the affiant got closer, she could smell a strong odor of alcohol. The defendant tried to explain that he was a law student just trying to go home. The defendant said that he didn't drive his car but borrowed his friend's bike to get home instead. The affiant performed three field sobriety tests, and the defendant failed all of them. The affiant placed the defendant under arrest for operating a vehicle under the influence of alcohol in violation of Section 39–18–504. The defendant started to cry.*

The defendant was then transported by the affiant to the Police Department for booking and processing.

Signed: <u>Patricia Anderson</u>
Patricia Anderson

Personally sworn to and subscribed by the affiant before me this day.

It appearing that the offense of Driving Under the Influence, a Class A misdemeanor has been committed by the defendant, and it appearing from said affidavit that there is probable cause that the defendant violated Section 39–18–504, this judge commands the arrest of the defendant and the defendant's appearance at the next possible court setting.

Signed: <u>**David Weddington**</u>
Magistrate Judge

**STATE WARRANT:** #171068

### ▶ Trial Testimony

The State called Baxter's friend, Rachel Nixon to the stand. Nixon threw a law school party at her house, and Baxter was there drinking bourbon all night. This is an excerpt of her testimony:

**Prosecutor:** *Can you describe the gathering at your house?*

**Ms. Nixon:** *Sure. It was pretty casual. We were having a little reunion of our law school 1L section. About 30 of my classmates were there. It was a potluck so people brought food to share, and I supplied the beer, wine, and bourbon. Justin came around 9 p.m. He is one of my closest guy friends at school.*

. . .

**Prosecutor:** *You testified earlier that you stopped Justin Baxter from getting into his car. Why?*

**Ms. Nixon:** *Oh, Justin had been drinking for hours at that point. It was about midnight, and I heard him mumble that he needed to go because he had an appointment on Friday morning with a professor about his clinic cases. But he looked a little unsteady on his feet. I don't remember a ton from my criminal law class, but I remember that having a DUI on your record wouldn't be good for his bar application.*

**Prosecutor:** *So what did you do next?*

**Ms. Nixon:** *I stopped him before he got to the door and told him not to drive. I knew he did not live far. He just lives down Main Street. So I suggested that he use my bike, which was in the garage. He thanked me at least ten times while I walked him to the bike.*

**Prosecutor:** *Can you describe the bike for us?*

**Ms. Nixon:** *Of course. My parents bought it for me when I came here for college. You know, five years ago. It's pink and neon green. It is a basic street bike, not a mountain bike or a racing bike. I remember that Justin laughed when he saw the bell and the basket.*

**Prosecutor:** *No further questions. Your witness.*

. . .

The testimony of the State's main witness, Officer Patricia Anderson, was consistent with what she stated in the Affidavit of Complaint above.

## ▶ Relevant Appellate Court Opinion

### Holden v. State

(2015)

WHITE, Court of Appeals Judge: Lily Holden appeals her conviction for operating a vehicle under the influence of alcohol (commonly know as "DUI"), in violation of Section 39–18–504 of the Criminal Code. Holden admitted that she smoked marijuana with her friends before taking her kayak out onto the Lake Louden. But she appeals her conviction arguing that using a kayak while under the influence of alcohol or drugs is not covered by Section 39–18–504. Unanimously, this three appellate judge panel finds that a kayak is not a vehicle as contemplated by the statute. This appeal presents an issue of first impression.

#### I. Statement of Facts

At approximately 6:30 p.m., Holden was in Loudon Park with a group of friends, and they were smoking marijuana. Holden decided to take her kayak out onto the water. There were several dozen people who were swimming in the lake, and one swimmer alerted a city police officer to Holden's unusual behavior. Officer Tim Plank testified at the preliminary hearing that when he reached the shore of the lake, he observed Holden "ramming into the large rocks on the east end of the lake." She was having a difficult time rowing and "turned the kayak over twice." He blew his whistle and signaled her to bring the kayak in. As she painstakingly rowed in, she did not appear to notice that she hit two swimmers. They were not in any way hurt by the kayak.

As Holden slowly pulled the kayak onto the shore, Officer Plank testified that he approached her and "smelled a strong odor of marijuana." Her eyes looked "bloodshot and sleepy," and "her speech was slurred." She told him that she was "hungry and needed a snack." Officer Plank determined that Holden was intoxicated and told her to keep the boat out of the water. He asked her to call someone to pick her up. Holden pointed to her friends on the other side of the lake. She said she would ask them for help and proceeded to put the kayak back in the water. When she did not stop at Officer Plank's suggestion, he arrested her for violating Section 39–18–504, signaling to her friends to come and retrieve the kayak.

### II. Is a kayak a "vehicle" under the DUI statute?

On appeal, Holden argues that Section 39–18–504 of the Criminal Code, which criminalizes operating a "vehicle" under the influence of marijuana, does not apply to her use of a kayak on Lake Loudon because a kayak is not a vehicle under the statute. Holden pleaded guilty but reserved her right to challenge the legal interpretation of the statute in defining a kayak as a vehicle on appeal.

The issue whether a kayak is a "vehicle" under Section 39–18–504 of the Criminal Code is a matter of statutory interpretation. In 1923, the Supreme Court explained that "[c]ourts should assume that the legislature means what it says and says what it means." *First American Trust v. Washington, 202 U.S. 145 (1923)*. As this Court stated in *Jones v. State* in 1978: "The words of a statute should be construed narrowly according to the meaning commonly attributed to them."

Here, the plain meaning of Section 39–18–504 is clear. It, provides, in relevant part, that it is illegal for a person under the influence of alcohol or drugs to "be in physical control of any vehicle." Section 39–18–504 (1) The definition section of the Criminal Code, however, defines a vehicle as "any appliance, including automobiles, street cars, or wagons pulled by beasts of burden that transports people from one place to another." Section 39-18-100. Given the clear and unambiguous language defining "vehicle," we therefore agree with Holden. A kayak is not an "appliance" like a car or even a horse-drawn wagon.

This statutory definition of vehicle is consistent with the Merriam-Webster Dictionary definition of a vehicle as "a machine that is used to carry people or things from one place to another." A kayak is in no way a machine. It has no moving parts, and does not use mechanical energy. In addition, the dictionary definition of kayak supports our conclusion—a kayak is "a long narrow boat that is pointed at both ends and that is moved by a paddle with two blades."

Furthermore, excluding kayaks from our statutory definition of vehicles is consistent with the legislative purpose of regulating traffic for the protection of the public. It stretches the imagination to declare that operating a kayak while intoxicated could seriously harm swimmers and other boat operators. This case is an example of that. Two swimmers went unharmed when Holden's kayak bumped into them. A kayak does not travel at high speeds like a car or have the power of a horse drawn wagon. Both of those vehicles have the capacity to cause serious bodily harm and even death to others.

### III. Conclusion

Giving effect to the clear statutory language of Section 39–18–504 (1), we find that the trial court erred in finding Holden guilty for operating a vehicle under the influence.

For the foregoing reasons, the judgment of the trial court is hereby reversed.

*So ordered.*

**▶ Exercise**

You represent either the State or Justin Baxter, as assigned by your professor. Prepare a five-minute oral argument about whether a bike is a vehicle under § 39–18–504 using solely the materials in the case file.

 **Points to Consider**

1. **Brief the case:** *Holden v. State* **(above).** What is the rule the court adopts? What is the court's rationale? What facts matter most to the Court of Appeals? Keep in mind that the same appellate judges will be deciding your case.

2. **Define the legal rule.** What legal rule are you trying to get the Court of Appeals to adopt? Write out the rule and use it to guide your opening sentence. In oral argument, judges want you to clearly state the issue and the rule that your legal argument and facts support.

3. **Identify your legal arguments and your legal authority.** Begin by using the outline on the next page to help you list your legal arguments. The legal issue in this case involves statutory interpretation. What rules of statutory interpretation will you use to support your arguments about the definition of a vehicle? What legal and non-legal persuasive authorities might assist you? Consider the legal arguments that Judge White of the Court of Appeals uses in *Holden v. State*. List as many arguments and sources of authority as you can. How can these arguments help your case? How can or should *Holden v. State* be distinguished from your case?

4.  **Use facts from your case to support your legal argument.** What facts matter to the legal issue? Some facts will be more central to your argument than others.

5.  **Predict the opposing side's strongest arguments and how you will rebut them.** Figuring out what the other side is going to say will help you refine your legal argument. What legal rule does the opposing side want the court to adopt and what arguments support that rule? Once you see the other side's position, you can make a list of rebuttal arguments so you are better prepared to address the judges' questions.

6.  **Outline the Oral Argument.** Use the Oral Argument Plan on the next page to help you prepare for the oral argument.

7.  **Conclusion.** Draft a concise and clear sentence to conclude your argument. Your goal is to end strong by summing up your argument in a memorable way for the judges.

# Your Oral Argument Plan

A.　Rule that you are asking the Court to adopt:

B.　Opening sentence for the Court:

C.　Present short outline for your argument (i.e. "Three legal arguments support this position. First, … Second, … Third …")

D.　Legal Argument Outline:

　1. Legal Argument:

　　a.　Supporting Authority

　　b.　Supporting Fact(s)

2. Legal Argument:

    a.    Supporting Authority

    b.    Supporting Fact(s)

3. Legal Argument:

    a.    Supporting Authority

    b.    Supporting Fact(s)

E.    Rebuttal of the Opposing Side's Argument

- Point 1

- Point 2

- Point 3

F.    Conclusion

# CHAPTER 2

# Punishment

## *Deciding Appropriate Punishment Through Plea Negotiations*

The contents of the relevant case file are as follows:

## ▶ Police Report

City Police Department

Incident Report

Report No. 5251954 Entered: July 21

Officer Badge No. 7443

On July 21, at approximately 2130 hours, this officer responded to a 911 cell phone call at the intersection of Volunteer Boulevard and 17th Street. Encountered the victim, Jeremy Charles, who was sitting on the curb. Victim is a 72-year-old African American man, and he was visibly shaken. Stated that unknown assailant approached from behind, put a pointed object into his back and shouted "give me all your damn money!" Victim then held his wallet out, assailant grabbed it, pushed victim down, and ran west on 17th Street. Charles said wallet contained credit cards, identification, and "maybe $45 in cash."

Other responding patrol vehicle encountered suspect, Alex "Shorty" Long, a Caucasian man, running along 17th Street near Cumberland Avenue. Suspect tossed object into bushes. Later retrieved and found to be wallet of victim. Victim later confirmed all cash and cards intact. Suspect brought to this officer for further investigation. Victim had only briefly seen suspect as he ran from scene, but indicated "looked and sounded like him."

Upon questioning, suspect confessed to crime and broke down crying. Suspect appeared to be intoxicated or high. Said he was "broke and needed money for pills." Further stated he "wasn't going to hurt anyone." Other officers stated that suspect was known to them as a homeless resident of the neighborhood.

Criminal check on suspect Long revealed three prior misdemeanor charges, two for public intoxication and one for disorderly conduct. The two public intoxication charges were dismissed. Guilty plea with sentence of time served on disorderly charge.

Suspect arrested for robbery and transported to detention center for processing.

## ▶ Indictment

### GRAND JURY INDICTMENT

No. <u>2527</u>

**STATE V. ALEXANDER LONG**

Charge:       ROBBERY—Felony
                Section 39–14–401
Court:        Sixth Judicial District Criminal Court

THE GRAND JURY, for the County of Manning, State of Volunteer, duly selected, impaneled, and sworn, upon their oaths find that:

#### ALEXANDER LONG

Hereinafter the defendant, on or about July 21st, in the County of Manning did intentionally and knowingly take and exercise control over the property of Jeremy Charles without consent and through violence and fear by the defendant using what by display the victim reasonably believed to be a dangerous weapon, against the peace and dignity of the State.

_____
Foreperson

▶ **Medical Records**

## VA VETERANS AFFAIRS

**Progress Notes**

Patient: Alexander Long
Physician: Dr. Henry Morgan

**Date: February 22**

Patient previously treated for alcoholism and self-reported addiction to hydrocodone. Previously referred for psychological assessment.

Diagnosis: PTSD disorder per criteria in DSM V. Five of eight criteria met. Patient self-medicating through use of alcohol and pain medications (not prescribed).

Treatment: Referred for out-patient treatment. Should patient not respond or become non-compliant, recommendation for in-patient rehabilitation and counseling.

**Date: May 25**

Patient ceased participation in treatment and not responding to outreach. Recommend in-patient referral if and when patient seeks care.

▶ **Applicable Statutes**

### § 39–11–102. Purposes.

1. The general purposes of the provisions governing the sentencing and treatment of offenders are:

a.  to prevent the commission of offenses;

b.  to promote the correction and rehabilitation of offenders;

c.  to punish offenders for violation of the law and societal interests;

d.  to safeguard offenders against excessive, disproportionate or arbitrary punishment;

e.  to give fair warning of the nature of the sentences that may be imposed on conviction of an offense;

f.  to differentiate among offenders with a view to a just individualization in their treatment .

## § 39-14-102. Theft.

A person is guilty of theft if he unlawfully takes, or exercises unlawful control over, movable property of another with purpose to deprive him thereof.

Theft of property less than $1000 in value is a misdemeanor, punishable by up to 11 months and 29 days incarceration plus a fine of up to $500.

## § 39–14–401. Robbery.

Robbery is the intentional or knowing theft of property from the person of another by violence or putting the person in fear.

Robbery of property under $1000 in value is a felony punishable by 2 to 4 years incarceration plus a fine of up to $5000.

### ▶ Exercise

Playing your assigned role as the prosecutor handling this case, or as Mr. Long's defense lawyer in this matter, complete the necessary preparation and planning for a scheduled meeting to discuss possible resolution of this case through a plea agreement for a specific sentence. Once prepared, conduct the negotiation. Be prepared to report on the results of your negotiation to your professor and the class.

 ## Points to Consider:

1. **Goals of Proposed Sentence.** Consider how your proposed sentence and that of opposing counsel advance, or not, the recognized purposes of criminal punishment. Do those goals change depending on your assigned role? Can you anticipate the justifications behind the proposal of your opposing counsel?

2. **Negotiation Style and Strategy.** Carefully consider the negotiation style you plan to use with the opposing counsel and why. Should you make the first offer? Does it matter that both the prosecutor and defense counsel are repeat players, regularly dealing with each other on cases?

3. **Role of Client and Witnesses.** How and when should defense counsel communicate with Mr. Long? Should the prosecutor speak with Mr. Charles? How and about what?

# Negotiation Plan

## State v. Long

### Law and Facts

    a.  Offense Statutes

    b.  Sentencing Statute

    c.  Analysis of facts

### Possible Arguments

    1.  What crime should form the basis of plea? Theft? Robbery?

      a.  What will my opponent say?

      b.  What is my position?

*Negotiation Plan, continued*

2. What should the sentence be?

   a. What should my position be?

      — Why? What justifications can I offer?

   b. What will my opponent say?

      — Why? What justifications will likely be offered?

      — How should I respond?

# CHAPTER 3

# Mens Rea

*Legal Drafting: Rewrite a Statute*

Thurman v. State

**ON YOUR WAY** to work, you check your email on your phone and are surprised to find an email from State Senator Meagan Wills in your inbox. You have only been a legal intern for her for three weeks and usually your assignments come from Joe Norris, the Senior Policy Research Advisor. You can't wait so you open it to find:

To: You
From: Senator Meagan Wills
Subject: Urgent: Draft Legislation Needed

Joe told me that you were responsible for the legal analysis in the speech that I gave to the State Bar yesterday. Specifically, your analysis of the Supreme Court's 4th Amendment decisions this term was really thorough and on point. Great work!

As my father used to say, though, no good deed goes unpunished. So this next assignment might require an all-nighter. The majority of my peers in the House and Senate are furious about the State Supreme Court's decision in *Thurman v. State*, which just came down last week. House Rep. Jessica Fitzsimons described it in news coverage on WNBC as "an unnecessary perversion of an important criminal statute—the unlawful possession of a loaded weapon."

I've attached the *Thurman* decision here and included the relevant statutes to save you time. I haven't had time to digest the entire opinion, but here is what I am frustrated with. The Supreme Court decided that the defendant should be punished for having a loaded gun even though the prosecution did not prove that the defendant knew it was loaded. They just presented a gun expert to say that it was in fact a loaded firearm. The court thinks that the statute lacks a mental culpability requirement for that element. I don't think that's what the legislators meant at the time they passed the law in 1972.

The bottom line is that I took criminal law over 30 years ago. And as a tax lawyer, I haven't had to think about words like mens rea since the bar exam. I figured that since you just finished your 1L year that you are best equipped to rewrite this statute to include a mens rea element for each material element.

I need a draft by tomorrow so I can circulate it to other legislators whose votes I'll need. Also, the NRA lobbyist has asked for a meeting and I'd like something to show him. Plus, I think this move will boost my ratings for my upcoming reelection bid. I look forward to seeing the draft bill in my inbox by 7 a.m. tomorrow morning.

—M.W.

## ▶ Applicable Statutes

### § 39–17–302. Definitions of Culpable Mental States.

a.   A person acts intentionally, or with intent, with respect to the nature of his conduct or to a result of his conduct when it is his conscious objective or desire to engage in the conduct or cause the result

b.   A person acts knowingly, or with knowledge, with respect to the nature of his conduct or to circumstances surrounding his conduct when he is aware of the nature of his conduct or that the circumstances exist. A person acts knowingly, or with knowledge, with respect to a result of his conduct when he is aware that his conduct is reasonably certain to cause the result.

c.    A person acts recklessly, or is reckless, with respect to circumstances surrounding his conduct or the result of his conduct when he is aware of but consciously disregards a substantial and unjustifiable risk that the circumstances exist or the result will occur. The risk must be of such a nature and degree that its disregard constitutes a gross deviation from the standard of care that an ordinary person would exercise under all the circumstances as viewed from the actor's standpoint.

d.    A person acts with criminal negligence, or is criminally negligent, with respect to circumstances surrounding his conduct or the result of his conduct when he ought to be aware of a substantial and unjustifiable risk that the circumstances exist or the result will occur. The risk must be of such a nature and degree that the failure to perceive it constitutes a gross deviation from the standard of care that an ordinary person would exercise under all the circumstances as viewed from the actor's standpoint.

### § 39–17–1301. Definitions.

In this chapter:

"Firearm" means any device designed, made, or adapted to expel a projectile through a barrel by using the energy generated by an explosion or burning substance or any device readily convertible to that use.

### § 39–17–1307. Unlawful Possession of a Weapon.

a.    A person commits a criminal offense if the person knowingly possesses a club, sword, illegal knife, or firearm.

b.    An offense under this section is Class A misdemeanor punishable by a fine up to $500, up to 1 year in prison, or both.

### § 39–17–1308. Unlawful Possession of a Loaded Weapon.

a.    A person commits a criminal offense if the person knowingly possesses a firearm and:

    (i)  that firearm is loaded, and

    (ii)  that person does not have a license to carry said firearm.

b.    Except as provided by Subsection (c), an offense under this section is a Class D felony punishable by a fine up to $4000, up to five years in prison, or both.

c.    An offense under this section is Class A misdemeanor if the offense is committed on the person's property and is punishable by a $500 fine.

▶ Relevant State Supreme Court Opinion

# Thurman v. State

AARONS, SUPREME COURT CHIEF JUSTICE:

Nathaniel Thurman appeals his conviction for possessing a loaded weapon in violation of Penal Code Section 39–17–1308. Section 39–17–1308 makes it a felony if a person "knowingly possesses" a firearm if that "firearm is loaded." The question in this case is one of proper statutory interpretation. Does the knowledge requirement under Section 39–17–1308(a) apply only to the possession of the firearm or does it also extend to the element in 39–17–1308(a)1308(a)(i) that the firearm was loaded? In short, does the defendant have to have knowledge that the object was in fact loaded, which the State would then be required to prove beyond a reasonable doubt? We conclude that the knowing mental state only attaches to the possession of the firearm element and not to the separate element in Section 39–17–1308(a)(i).

## I. Facts of the Case

Nathaniel Thurman, the defendant, is a fifty-five-year-old father of four who worked as a handyman at Bayside High School. On the night of his arrest at about 5:30 p.m., he was on his way to meet his family at his parent's house for Wednesday night supper. As he was walking out the door, he grabbed his father's Revolutionary War pistol to return it to him. The defendant's father testified at trial that he asked his son to have this family heirloom appraised for him.

The defendant took the pistol from his home and placed it in the passenger's seat of his car. On the way to his parent's house, he failed to come to a complete stop at the stop sign at the intersection of 21st Street and Massachusetts Avenue. Officer Buchannon pulled over the defendant's vehicle and approached the car. As he asked for the defendant's license and registration, he noticed the gun in the passenger's seat. Although the defendant tried to explain why he had the pistol, Officer Buchannon said that he had no choice but to arrest him for a weapon in plain view. The defendant had admitted to Officer Buchannon that he did not have a license for it. But the defendant testified that he did not know that the pistol was loaded.

A firearms expert testified at the trial that the pistol was indeed an historical Revolutionary War flintlock pistol. Specifically, this pistol was manufactured by the Pennsylvania Gun Safety Factory in Lancaster, Pennsylvania in February 1776 and bore 5th Company Huntington Regiment Markings. Although on cross-examination the expert admitted that the pistol was probably inoperable, he verified that it was loaded at the time it was recovered by Officer Buchannon.

## II. Legal Analysis

After the state rested, Thurman moved to dismiss for insufficient proof that he had knowledge that the pistol was loaded. The defendant argued that the language under Section 39–17–1308 is clear. It requires knowledge that he was in possession of a firearm, and knowledge that the firearm was loaded. Essentially, a knowing mens rea applies to each element of the statute.

The trial judge denied the motion, and the Court of Appeals affirmed. We agree with the rationale of the Court of Appeals and affirm.

As is clear from the plain language of the statute, the knowledge requirement only applies only to the words that directly follow it—possesses a firearm. To find a person guilty of Section 39–17–1308, the State must prove: first, that the defendant had knowledge that he was in possession of a firearm; second, that the firearm was loaded, and third, that the person did not have a license to the firearm. Looking at the construction of the statute, the legislature separated out the element that the "firearm is loaded" into its own section, 39–17–1308. This is a clear signal that the knowledge requirement does not apply to 39–17–1308(i), making the fact that the firearm is loaded a strict liability element.

Our jurisdiction, unlike other states, has no default rules that disfavor strict liability or presumptively distributes any culpability term appearing in the definition of the offense to all material elements. For example, New York passed two default rules that parallel the Model Penal Code default rules under MPC 2.02(1) and 2.02(4). New York Penal Law 15.15(2) requires clear legislative intent to apply strict liability to any element of an offense, and

New York Penal Law 15.15(1) distributes any mental state in a statute to all elements unless clearly stated otherwise. Under any criminal statute in New York, unless the statute expressly states that strict liability applies, a person must have at least acted negligently. We have neither default rule to invoke.

Finally, even a practical reading of the possession of a loaded weapon statute supports this interpretation. It would be nearly impossible for the state to prove beyond a reasonable doubt that the defendant knew the gun was loaded, which would make the statute virtually unenforceable.

This interpretation of the statute is also consistent with Section 39–17–1307 which creates a lesser offense for possessing a firearm that is not loaded. We discern a clear legislative intent to leave the material element that the firearm is loaded without a required culpable mental state. The State, therefore, satisfied their burden to prove the elements of the offense.

*The order of the Court of Appeals is upheld.*

## ▶ Exercise

Draft an amendment to the unlawful carrying of a loaded weapon statute that fixes the mens rea problem created by the Supreme Court decision.

Senator Wills dropped by your office to explain what she hoped your amended statute would achieve. She does not want any material element to be interpreted as a strict liability element. There should be a required mental state that is clear for each element. So your amended statute should reflect that.

Use the template below to help you draft the changes and consider the following points before you begin drafting.

Points to Consider

1. **Mens Rea for § 39–17–1308:**

   a.    How can the statute be amended to require some level of mental culpability related to the loaded nature of the gun? Should it be a knowledge requirement or something else? What other options do you have?

   b.    Would a knowledge requirement run into the problem that Chief Justice Aarons predicts? Could the prosecution prove that the defendant knew the gun was loaded? Could circumstantial evidence or an inference be sufficient?

2. **Mental State Default Rules.** Should you draft additional statutes that mirror the default rules in both the Model Penal Code and New York Penal Law? Look up New York Penal Law 15.15(1) and 15.15(2). Weigh the advantages and disadvantages of such legislation.

3. **Your judgment.** Do you agree or disagree with Senator Wills' opinion? How can your views about gun control laws impact the drafting choices you make for amending this legislation? Should they?

4. **Draft the Statute(s).** Use the Model Senate Bill below to help you draft the new legislation.

## Drafting Practice

Amended Penal Code § 39–17–1308—Unlawful Possession of a
Loaded Weapon.

Mark up the statute with the changes you want to propose:

**§ 39–17–1308. Unlawful Possession of a Loaded Weapon.**

    a.    A person commits a criminal offense if the person knowingly possesses a firearm and:

        (i)  that firearm is loaded, and

        (ii)  that person does not have a license to carry said firearm.

The new statute should read:

*Drafting Practice, continued*

**New Penal Code § 39–17–1328—Default Mental Culpability Rule(s)**

The new statute should read:

***HOUSE BILL 4193***
*By Rep. Fagan*

## SENATE BILL 3585

By Senator Wills

*AN ACT to amend Penal Code § Sec. 39–17–1308. Unlawful Possession of a Loaded Weapon.\**

*BE IT ENACTED BY THE GENERAL ASSEMBLY OF THIS STATE:*

*SECTION 1. Penal Code § Sec. 39–17–1308() is amended by adding*

_____

_____

_____

_____

*SECTION 2. Penal Code § Sec. 39–17–1308() is amended by adding*

_____

_____

_____

_____

*SECTION 3. Penal Code § Sec. 39–17–1308() is amended by adding*

_____

_____

_____

_____

*\* Note: You may not need this many additions or deletions from the statute. They are only provided to help you see how to draft the statute.*

*SECTION 4. Penal Code § Sec. 39–17–1308() is amended by deleting*

_____

_____

_____

_____

SECTION 5. Penal Code § Sec. 39–17–1308() is amended by deleting

_____

_____

_____

_____

*SECTION 6. Penal Code § Sec. 39–17–1308() is amended by deleting*

_____

_____

_____

_____

*SECTION 7. Penal Code § Sec. 39–17–1308() is amended by*

_____

_____

_____

_____

SECTION_____. This act shall take effect upon becoming a law, the public welfare requiring it.

# CHAPTER 4

# Actus Reus

## *Interviewing and Counseling a Client*

To: You, Associate

From: Paula Sharper, Partner

**CONGRATULATIONS** *on your jury trial victory in the Johnson case. Acquittals are hard to come by in this business. Based on your great work to date, I need you to handle a new matter. I am getting ready for trial next week so I cannot focus on this new case, which is fairly time sensitive.*

*I received a call from Nicki Sampson. She is a divorced mother with an eight-year-old daughter, Jesse. About six months ago, Jesse was diagnosed with Hodgkin's lymphoma, a very treatable form of cancer especially in children. In fact, with treatment the five-year survival rate for children is 97 percent. If the cancer is untreated, the overall five-year survival rate is less than 5 percent.*

*About the same time as Jesse was diagnosed, Ms. Sampson joined the New Horizons Faith Church. New Horizons is an independent, non-denominational church whose tenets include, among other things, a commitment to faith healing and an aversion to any modern medical treatment.*

*The church is led by a charismatic preacher, Harry Powell. Preacher Powell encouraged Ms. Sampson to put her faith in God to heal her daughter. He assisted by holding her while Nicki and the entire church prayed. Those "treatments" occurred every Wednesday and Sunday for the last three months.*

*Jesse, however, continues to decline. In response to a report from a neighbor of the Sampsons, the Department of Children Services has initiated an investigation and has met with Ms. Sampson once already. They are considering pursuing criminal mistreatment charges.*

*Ms. Sampson has scheduled an appointment for tomorrow. I did a little preliminary research and have attached a couple relevant statutes. It appears that she may fall within the "religious belief" exception for mistreatment. But that exception does not appear to apply beyond the mistreatment statute as you can see from the excerpt from a recent case I have also attached.*

*Please meet with Ms. Sampson, interview her and advise her regarding the DCS investigation and her decision regarding traditional medical treatment, or not, for her daughter.*

## ▶ Applicable Statutes

### § 39–13–115. Criminal Mistreatment.

1. A person commits the crime of criminal mistreatment in the second degree if, with criminal negligence and:

   a. In violation of a legal duty to provide care for another person, the person withholds necessary and adequate food, physical care or medical attention from that person; or

    b.  Having assumed the permanent or temporary care, custody or responsibility for the supervision of another person, the person withholds necessary and adequate food, physical care or medical attention from that person.

2.  A person commits the crime of criminal mistreatment in the first degree if, with criminal intent or knowledge, and:

    a.  In violation of a legal duty to provide care for another person, the person withholds necessary and adequate food, physical care or medical attention from that person; or

    b.  Having assumed the permanent or temporary care, custody or responsibility for the supervision of another person, the person withholds necessary and adequate food, physical care or medical attention from that person.

3.  As used in this section, "legal duty" includes but is not limited to a duty created by familial relationship, court order, contractual agreement, statute or case law.

4.  This section does not apply to a person who provides a dependent person with spiritual treatment through prayer from a duly accredited practitioner of spiritual treatment, in lieu of medical treatment, in accordance with the tenets of a recognized church or religious denomination of which the parent or guardian of the dependent person is a member or an adherent.

### § 39–13–203. Second Degree Murder.

Second degree murder is a knowing killing of another.

### § 39–13–205. Involuntary Manslaughter.

Involuntary manslaughter is the reckless killing of another.

### § 39–13–206. Criminally Negligent Homicide.

Criminally negligent homicide is criminally negligent conduct that results in death.

▶ **Case Excerpt**

## State v. Kimble

### (2005)

Defendant is a member of the Church of the First Born, a small Pentecostal denomination that has approximately 12,000 to 15,000 members throughout the country. An essential tenet of the denomination is that God is operational in the life of each believer, including when he or she is sick. According to church doctrine, if members pray for one who is ill, God will honor those prayers and restore the member to health. The church permits the use of purely corrective devices, such as eyeglasses or crutches, and it allows its members to undergo medical examinations when required. It does not, however, allow medical treatment.

Defendant is a long-time member of the church and is one of the three elders of the congregation in Greenville, where he lives. He has never in his life taken a pill or received an injection, although at times he has suffered excruciating pain.

Defendant's eight-year-old son, Bobby, became ill in October 2004. After a temporary improvement in his condition on his return, Bobby's condition became considerably worse. At the child's request, defendant and the other elders of the church prayed over him. By the end of October, defendant suspected, based on his reading of medical literature, that Bobby was suffering from leukemia. The next morning the elders again prayed over the child, who died in defendant's arms soon afterwards. According to the record, leukemia in children is readily treatable, with a 98 percent chance of remission after a month of treatment and a 70 to 85 percent chance of survival for at least a significant number of years. There is little chance of survival for untreated leukemia; death from the disease involves severe pain.

* * * *

Section 39–13–115(4) provides an exception to the criminal mistreatment statute for:

> [A] a person who provides a dependent person with spiritual treatment through prayer from a duly accredited practitioner of spiritual treatment in lieu of medical treatment, in accordance with the tenets of a recognized church or religious denomination of which the parent or guardian of the dependent person is a member or an adherent.

A person who treats a dependent child through prayer, thus, has a defense to a charge of criminal mistreatment. The defense, however, does not apply to a charge of criminally negligent homicide. Thus, so long as the child does not die, the parent has a defense to a criminal charge; once the child dies, the defense is gone.

 ## Points to Consider

1. **Preparation for the Interview.** It is always advisable to think through and plan for the interview. For example, you may want to prepare an outline of the major topics you need to cover, including the order in which you want to cover them.

2. **Conducting the Interview.** Although you want to be prepared, you need to be flexible during the interview so that you can respond and follow up on information provided by the client. Normally open-ended questions (starting with who, what, why, when, where, explain, describe) are the most effective. You need to establish rapport from the outset, so questions designed to get to know the client and break the ice may be helpful. Waiting on the more sensitive subjects until later in the interview is often advisable. While you need to take some notes to keep a record of what you learn, you should not let note-taking interfere with the conversation or flow of the interview. You can always draft a detailed summary after the client leaves.

3. **Advising and Counseling the Client.** You also need to think through any advice or counseling you may offer the client. As a new attorney, you will want to answer all of your client's questions, but beware: off the cuff advice can be wrong and often creates problems down the road. Saying "I do not know the exact answer to that question" or "I will need to research that question further" is the best way to go in that situation. So take the time to look at the applicable statutes of the case and consider what options Ms. Sampson may have in advance of interviewing her. In this time-sensitive case where a child's health is at issue, you may want to provide some preliminary advice during the interview. Counseling advice is often presented with the pros and cons of the alternative proposed decisions or courses of action.

Alternatively, you may want to first interview the client and gather as much information about the client and the circumstances as possible. This ensures that you have enough time to assess fully and do any needed research before providing advice to the client. You can then schedule a second session with the client to provide the analysis and advice.

4. **Well Being of the Child.** What is your role and responsibility with regard to the child? How does that affect how you approach the interview? How does it affect the advice and counsel you may provide? Are your personal feelings relevant? If so, how? If not, how you handle any conflict between your views and the views of Ms. Sampson? Or is your role simply to discuss the legal implications?

5. **Follow Up.** You should consider outlining for Ms. Sampson any action that you plan to take in light of the interview. Are there additional legal issues that you need to research? Any facts that you want to investigate before your next meeting? You should also outline the tasks, if any, that Ms. Sampson may need to undertake based on the interview. Normally you should also follow up with a written summary of those actions, tasks, and any advice you provided during the interview.

## Your Interview Plan

A.  Introductions

B.  Topic Outline

1.

2.

3.

4.

5.

6.

C.  Possible Advice

D.  Follow-Up Actions

## Your Interview Notes

Date:

Attorney-Client Privileged
Attorney Work Product

# Counseling Plan

1.  Possible Course of Action A

    A.  Pros

    B.  Cons

    C.  Other Considerations

2.  Possible Course of Action B

    A.  Pros

    B.  Cons

    C.  Other Considerations

*Counseling Plan, continued*

### 3. Possible Course of Action C

    A.  Pros

    B.  Cons

    C.  Other Considerations

# CHAPTER 5

# Homicide
*Drafting: Recommend an Appropriate*
*Charge to Supervising Attorney*

**THE DISTRICT ATTORNEY,** your boss, assigns you a new case to investigate.

## ▶ Case Investigation

**1. Your first step is to interview the investigating officer,** Gus Grimly, who tells you the following:

> At approximately 5:10 pm yesterday, Officer Grimly responded to several 911 calls about a shooting at 310 S. Desoto Street in the Beverly Hills area of Citrus County. The address is in a residential area where he found the victim, Marco Gonzalez, 44, a Mexican-American man, on the sidewalk. Mr. Gonzalez had been shot several times and was dead when Grimly arrived.

> Grimly learned that two men, Eric Boyle and Marco Gonzalez, became involved in an "aggressive driving incident" in the Citrus Hills area. Boyle, an African American man, 52, drove to his home off Desoto Street, then pulled into the driveway. Gonzalez was still behind Boyle by the time he arrived at his home. After Boyle pulled into his driveway, Gonzalez parked his car in front of the home. Boyle got out of his car and walked up to Gonzalez's car, which was also occupied by Gonzalez's wife, child, and grandson.

According to Grimly, Gonzalez got out of his car, telling his wife to stay in the passenger's seat, as Boyle was approaching him with a firearm. Witnesses said that Boyle fired a shot, paused briefly, fired another shot, paused again, and then fired quickly three times. Gonzalez fell to the ground as he was heading back to his vehicle. Boyle then approached Gonzalez's car with his firearm drawn and pointed it at the wife, daughter, and grandson. He made all three get out of the vehicle, then held them at gunpoint until law enforcement arrived at the scene..

After Boyle was placed under arrest and mirandized, he told Grimly that while he was driving home, he saw Gonzalez trying to force him off the road and "brake checking" him. Boyle said Gonzalez followed him all the way back to his house, and that when he got out of his car, Gonzalez threatened him. That was when Boyle said he removed his firearm from his pocket, loaded the chamber, and pointed the weapon at Gonzalez.

Gonzalez's wife, Cathy, told Grimly that Boyle was driving aggressively, and that they only went to his house to get his address to give to law enforcement. Once they arrived at Boyle's house, they saw him get out of his vehicle and immediately point a gun at them. To protect her and the kids, her husband got out of the car. She could not hear what he was saying to Boyle. But she then saw Boyle fire several gunshots at Gonzalez. Boyle then started walking toward her car and pointed the gun at her and her family. An independent witness who saw the shooting from about 75 yards away said he saw Boyle pointing the handgun at Gonzalez, and that Gonzalez was backing away when Boyle started shooting.

**2. You next obtain the transcripts of three 911 calls** related to the incident. One call is from Eric Boyle. One is from Cathy Gonzalez. And one call is from an unidentified witness.

### 911 Call—From Eric R. Boyle

Recording:
Thursday, Time is 5:05 pm.

**911:** *This is 911. What is the emergency?*

**Boyle:** *I have a truck, there's some maniac that's been following me, trying to run me off the (expletive) road. My gun is already out. It's cocked and locked. I am five blocks from my house.*

**911:** *Sir . . .*

**Boyle:** *He's following me there.*

**911:** *Roosevelt?*

**Boyle:** *Beverly Hills and they are following me to my house. I will be there in 20 seconds, and the gun is already out.*

**911:** *Sir, no.*

**Boyle:** *I am going home. The gun is coming out, and I am going to put it to his head.*

**Wife (in background):** *They are coming to our house. The police substation is right up the street. Drive there.*

**Boyle:** *Never any cops there.*

**Wife:** *We don't need to go to our house.*

**911:** *Where is the vehicle now?*

**Boyle:** *Right on my tail.*

**911:** *Hold on for me.*

**Boyle:** *Going down right now.*

**Wife:** *I can't even get the garage door open.*

**Boyle:** *You don't need to. Just throw it into park as soon as I am stopped.*

### 911 Call—From Cathy Gonzalez

Recording:
Thursday, July 23d, 2015. Time is 5:05 pm.

**911:** *This is 911. What is the emergency?*

**Gonzalez:** *A guy is driving like an idiot. What he did…he just cut off a Honda minivan. He is turning up Roosevelt. We live off Monroe. Somebody needs to smack the crap out of that idiot. My husband wants to whip his ass.*

**911:** *If he does that your husband will go to jail. What is your name ma'am?*

**Gonzalez:** *Cutting off people…[inaudible yelling].*

**911:** *I can't understand you with the screaming.*

**Gonzalez:** *We are just driving an old truck with a trailer. You just don't drive like that. He's an idiot.*

**911:** *I understand that, but I am just trying to get this information. I can't hear you over him.*

**Gonzalez:** *Oh now he has turned up. We're not going to follow him?*

**Husband:** *(in background) Yes we are. We need to get his address.*

**911:** *No. You need to go home.*

**Gonzalez:** *Okay, we are going home. Oh...I guess we aren't.*

**Husband:** *I have your number buddy...Son of a bitch has a gun!*

**Gonzalez:** *He's got a gun!*

**Gonzalez:** *Don't shoot! I have 911 on the phone.*

Shots heard.

**Gonzalez:** *Oh my God! He shot my husband. Please hurry!*

### 911 Call—From Witness

Recording:
Thursday, July 23d, 2015. Time is 5:12 pm.

**911:** *This is 911. What is the emergency?*

**Caller:** *On Desoto Street. Guy got shot. He's on the ground.*

**911:** *You said it's on Desoto?*

**Caller:** *Yes, ma'am. Guy just got shot.*

**911:** *What is your name?*

**Caller:** *[no response]*

**911:** *Do you know what happened?*

**Caller:** *I was just driving down the road. Saw a guy pointing a gun and saw him shoot another guy. His old lady is out of the truck now. It's a long truck. The guy was actually walking back to his truck when the dude shot him.*

**911:** *Is the long truck near the victim?*

**Caller:** *Yeah. I see his wife or whatever outside the truck. I see children getting out of the vehicle. He still has the guy at gun point. Probably shot him five times.*

## ▶ Applicable Statutes

### § 39–13–202. First Degree Murder.

First degree murder is:

1.   A premeditated, deliberate, and intentional killing of another, or

2.   A killing of another that occurs when a person is attempting or committing sexual assault of a child, aggravated criminal sexual assault, robbery, burglary, residential burglary, arson, aggravated arson, or aggravated kidnapping.

### § 39–13–203. Second Degree Murder.

Second degree murder is a knowing killing of another.

### § 39–13–204. Voluntary Manslaughter.

Voluntary manslaughter is the intentional or knowing killing of another in a state of passion produced by adequate provocation sufficient to lead a reasonable person to act in an irrational manner.

### § 39–13–205. Involuntary Manslaughter.

Involuntary manslaughter is the reckless killing of another.

### § 39-11-302. Definitions of Culpable Mental States.

A person acts intentionally, or with intent, with respect to the nature of his conduct or to a result of his conduct when it is his conscious objective or desire to engage in the conduct or cause the result

A person acts knowingly, or with knowledge, with respect to the nature of his conduct or to circumstances surrounding his conduct when he is aware of the nature of his conduct or that the circumstances exist. A person acts knowingly, or with knowledge, with respect to a result of his conduct when he is aware that his conduct is reasonably certain to cause the result.

A person acts recklessly, or is reckless, with respect to circumstances surrounding his conduct or the result of his conduct when he is aware of but consciously disregards a substantial and unjustifiable risk that the circumstances exist or the result will occur. The risk must be of such a nature and degree that its disregard constitutes a gross deviation from the standard of care that an ordinary person would exercise under all the circumstances as viewed from the actor's standpoint.

A person acts with criminal negligence, or is criminally negligent, with respect to circumstances surrounding his conduct or the result of his conduct when he ought to be aware of a substantial and unjustifiable risk that the circumstances exist or the result will occur. The risk must be of such a nature and degree that the failure to perceive it constitutes a gross deviation from the standard of care that an ordinary person would exercise under all the circumstances as viewed from the actor's standpoint.

### § 39–11–401. Self-Defense.

Use of force upon or toward another person is justifiable when the actor believes that such force is immediately necessary for the purpose of protecting himself against the use of unlawful force by such other person on the present occasion.

## ▶ Exercise

Based on your interview of Officer Grimly, your review of the 911 tapes, and your understanding of the applicable statutes, draft an email to your boss outlining what charges you think should be filed and the reasoning behind your recommendation. Read the following points to consider before drafting the email.

## Points to Consider:

1. **Explaining your legal analysis to the District Attorney.** Always consider the audience for your communication. Your boss knows the law fairly well and does not need a lot of citations to statutes and legal authority. She is interested in a brief review of the results of your investigation, your recommended charges, and a succinct explanation of your reasoning. Do you have any questions about the facts that might influence your recommendation?

2. **Case Resolution.**

   Recognize that most cases are resolved through negotiation to a plea bargain. If the case is likely to be resolved through negotiation, does that impact your recommendation?

   If the case is most likely to proceed to a jury trial, does that alter your recommendation? Explain your thinking on this issue briefly in the email.

3. **Prosecutorial discretion provides you with flexibility in your charging recommendation.** If you decide to charge Mr. Boyle with a lesser offense, what do you think can be proved? Explain your decision. If instead you decide to charge Mr. Boyle with the most serious crime you think you can prove, explain your decision.

## Prepare Your Email

From:    You
To:       District Attorney
Subject:  Recommended Charge in Eric Boyle Case

# CHAPTER 6

# Felony Murder
## *Drafting an Indictment*

**THE DISTRICT ATTORNEY** walks into your office and commends you on your big win in the Eric Boyle case. She says that your charging decisions made a huge difference in the outcome and that, especially for a young prosecutor, you show great strategic judgment.

The District Attorney then hands you a case file. It's a horrible situation. You first heard about it on the news a week ago. In the early morning, around 1 a.m., a two-story residence became engulfed in flames, and the fire killed eight-year-old Joseph McDermott and five-year-old Erica McDermott.

A thirty-two-year-old woman, Sara Henderson, has been arrested and confessed to setting a garbage can on fire outside the building. She was charged with arson several years ago, but the facts at the time didn't add up, and the case was dismissed. She has no other adult criminal record, but she has a juvenile record for shoplifting once when she was 16.

The District Attorney asks you to prepare an indictment and wants you to present the case to the grand jury next week. Because the case is getting so much press, she wants to look over the indictment first. You tell her that you'll have a draft on her desk in two days. Here are the case materials you have: the defendant's sworn statement, the relevant investigation memorandum from Detective McNulty, notes from your conversation with Dr. Shah, and the statutes that you need:

## ▶ Case Investigation

### Sworn Confession

After informing Sara Henderson of her constitutional rights, Detective McNulty interviewed her. He memorialized the interview with the following signed and sworn statement from Henderson:

> *I, Sara Henderson, do hereby swear that the following statement is a true and accurate depiction of the events described herein. I volunteer the following information, without duress, coercion or promise of immunity:*
>
> *At about midnight on the night of the fire, I got into a fight with my girlfriend, Sandra Thomas. After drinking and watching a movie, Sandra started to get onto me about our overdue rent. Money has always been a source of tension in our relationship. I started yelling. She told me that I needed to get second job, and that I just wasn't pulling my weight. That was the last straw. I picked up the glass that I was drinking from, threw it at her, and ran out of the house. I was furious, and looking for a way to blow off steam. I've had a problem since I was a kid with fire. I even went to therapy for it. But I have had it under control recently.*
>
> *So I walked only a block from my apartment to an open lot on West 25th Street toward two dumpsters and tried to light the trash on fire. It was way too windy. Nothing would ignite. Then I walked a few more blocks and saw a large garbage can between two houses. The garbage can was pretty far away from the place that caught on fire. I can't see how the fire in the cans would catch onto*

*anything. I knew the family that lived there. Our neighborhood
is pretty tight. I would never want to hurt anyone in that house. I
know kids live there. It was an accident. I am so sorry.*

*I used a lighter and a cigarette to start the fire. The flames started
to grow fast. I got scared and ran. I didn't want to get in trouble so
I didn't call 911. I wish I had. I never thought that the kids could get
hurt. I got in my car and went to my grandmother's house for the
night. She lives about 15 minutes away. I heard about the kids the
next morning and came here to explain what I did. I am so sorry
this all happened.*

## ▶ Office Memorandum from Detective McNulty

To:      You
From:    Detective McNulty
Re:      Henderson Case Notes

The following are interview summaries of potential grand jury and
trial witnesses (I also have detailed interview notes if you would like
to review them as well):

**Rhonda McDermott:** She explained that she lived on the second
floor of a two-story residence located at 2442 West 28th Street.
Her two children, Joseph and Erica, lived with her. Her mother,
sister, and nephew, live on the first floor. On the night of the fire,
she put the kids to bed at around 8:30 p.m. and went to meet her
boyfriend around 10:30 p.m. Her sister, Doris, texted her around
1:15 a.m. about a fire and told Rhonda to go to St. Vincent's
Hospital. When she got there, the doctors told her that there was
nothing they could do. Her children died in the fire.

**Doris McDermott:** She said that she knew she was watching the kids and that her sister went out around 10:30 p.m. She fell asleep shortly after her sister left. She awoke later that night and smelled smoke. She looked out of a window and saw that the back of the house was engulfed in flames. She woke her mother and son and got out of the house. She called the police on her cell. Once she left the residence, she realized that Rhonda's children were still in the house. As soon as the firefighters arrived, she told them that the kids were inside. She texted her sister to come home. She watched as they removed them through their bedroom window on the second floor. She followed the ambulance to the hospital.

When asked if there was gas or any explosive material near the house, Doris said that there were gas containers for the grill on the back porch. Other than that, there was nothing she could think of. She said that the garbage can was not near the house, but in the alley about 4 feet from the house. It was a large plastic garbage can, provided by the city, and shared by two of the residences on the street.

**Firefighter Ben Reynolds:** He responded to an alarm concerning the fire at 2442 West 28th Street. When Reynolds arrived at the scene, he said that it was very windy and very cold. The fire was going strong with heavy smoke. His team discovered intense flames from top to bottom in the back of the building. On the first floor, he saw the back porch burning. He did not see a garbage can burning in the alley. With the help of another firefighter, he got the children out of the second-floor apartment.

**Supervising Fire Marshal Spencer Conway:** He went to the scene of the fire and visually examined the debris. He explained that they were looking for evidence to corroborate defendant's confession. Specifically, they were looking for remnants of a garbage can. Once they reached the base-level, Connor could smell a very, very strong odor that smelled like gasoline. Accordingly, he took a sample of the soil, which he placed in a metal can and transported the can to the crime lab for analysis.

**Sandra Thomas:** She corroborated Henderson's story. The only thing she added was that Henderson was clinically depressed and took anti-depressant medicine. She has been together with Henderson for over four years, and although they get into fights, she said that this one was the worst yet. She also has seen Henderson light things on fire for fun, like newspaper and wood.

## ▶ Preliminary Autopsy Notes

Dr. Shah gave a preliminary report from the autopsies of Joseph and Erica McDermott. The external examination of both revealed the presence of soot around the nose and mouth. Moreover, there were various areas of skin slippage where their skin had severely blistered. The internal examination revealed soot on the tongue and trachea, a finding that is consistent with inhaling smoke from a fire. Toxicology tests were pending. Based on her review of the reports, Dr. Shah concluded that both died from carbon monoxide intoxication from the fire and that the manner of death was homicide.

## ▶ Applicable Statutes

The statutes covering degrees of homicide and culpable mental states can be found in Chapter Five. (See pages 62–64 for applicable statutes: §§ 39–13–202 through 39–13–205 and § 39–13–302.)

### § 39–13–301. Arson.

a.   A person commits arson when, by means of fire or explosive, he or she knowingly:

    1.   Damages any real property, or any personal property having a value of $150 or more, of another without his or her consent; or

    2.   With intent to defraud an insurer, damages any property or any personal property having a value of $150 or more.

b.   A person commits residential arson when he or she, in the course of committing arson, knowingly damages, partially or totally, any building or structure that is the dwelling place of another.

### § 39–13–302. Aggravated Arson.

a.   A person commits aggravated arson when in the course of committing arson he or she knowingly damages, partially or totally, any building or structure, including any adjacent building or structure, and:

    1.   the person knows or reasonably should know that one or more persons are present therein or

    2.   any person suffers great bodily harm, or permanent disability or disfigurement as a result of the fire or explosion.

▶ **Exercise**

After considering the points below, prepare the indictment for this case using the template that follows. List the counts that you plan to present to the grand jury.

 **Points to Consider**

1. **An Indictment.** An indictment is a written accusation that an individual has committed a criminal offense. The purpose of an indictment is to inform the defendant of the essential elements of the offense charged so that a person can prepare a defense.

   If the indictment charges more than one offense, each offense should be charged in a separate count. Although a prosecutor frames an indictment for the grand jury, the grand jury ultimately decides what counts, if any, will be listed in the indictment. A bill of indictment by a grand jury is called a true bill.

   Each jurisdiction has its own rules of Criminal Law that govern what needs to be included in an indictment. In your jurisdiction, Criminal Law Rule 7 states: "An indictment must be a plain, concise, and definite written statement of the essential facts constituting the offense charged and must be signed by an attorney for the state. For each count charged, the indictment must state the statute that the defendant has been alleged to violate and the essential elements required. The indictment shall be presented to the grand jury."

2. **Sample Count in an Indictment.** Before you begin, you look at an indictment in a recent burglary case to help you think about how to draft each count. Here is one example:

## COUNT ONE

### Aggravated Burglary

1.   On or about August 7th, Devon Bryant, a resident of this county, did enter the dwelling of Julie Groves.

1.   When Bryant entered the home of Julie Groves at least one person was inside the home.

2.   Bryant entered armed with a bat and a knife with the intent to remove the money and property of another.

3.   Bryant armed with a bat and a knife intended to assault Julie Groves.

4.   Bryant removed items belonging to Ms. Grove including an iPhone and jewelry from her home.

In violation of Section 39-14-405 of the Criminal Code.

---

3. **Legal Elements.** What counts will you bring against Ms. Henderson? List the counts and the essential elements before beginning to draft the indictment. Will you quote the exact language of the statute in its entirety? If not, how will you summarize the necessary elements that must be proved beyond a reasonable doubt?

4. **Facts.** What facts are necessary to your legal argument? You have a great deal of investigation started in this case. Your goal when writing the indictment is to meet the requirements of Criminal Law

Rule 7 without giving away too much of your preliminary investigation. What facts do you need? What facts do you want to exclude?

5. **Proximate Cause.** Your state has adopted a proximate cause approach to felony murder, which is followed by a minority of states. According to a 1943 case, *State v. Jackson,* "under the proximate-cause theory of liability, liability attaches under the felony murder rule for any death proximately resulting from the unlawful activity . . . When a person's attempt to commit a forcible felony sets in motion a chain of events which were or should have been within his contemplation when the motion was initiated, he should be held responsible for any death which by direct and almost inevitable sequence results from the initial criminal act." The majority of states follow the agency theory of liability for felony murder. Under this theory, felony murder only applies to a killing that is directly attributable to the act of the defendant or those associated with him in the criminal act. Does the applicable theory of liability matter in this case?

## Draft Indictment

**STATE CRIMINAL COURT**

STATE                    )
                         )
v.                       )    CASE NO. 022775
                         )    JUDGE SHIRLEY
HENDERSON                )
                         )

**INDICTMENT**

The Grand Jury charges as follows:

**COUNT ONE**
List Offense Charged Here

1. On or about          , SARA HENDERSON, a resident of this county, did

2.

3.

4.

In violation of Section          of the Criminal Code.

## COUNT TWO

List Offense Charged Here

1. On or about          , SARA HENDERSON, a resident of this county, did

2.

3.

4.

In violation of Section          of the Criminal Code.

## COUNT THREE

List Offense Charged Here

1. On or about          , SARA HENDERSON, a resident of this county, did

2.

3.

4.

In violation of Section          of the Criminal Code.

*Draft Indictment, continued*

## COUNT FOUR
### List Offense Charged Here

1. On or about _____ , SARA HENDERSON, a resident of this county, did

2.

3.

4.

In violation of Section _____ of the Criminal Code.

A TRUE BILL:

_____

GRAND JURY FOREPERSON

DEBRA SAWYER
DISTRICT ATTORNEY

By: _____
Your Name Here
Assistant District Attorney

# CHAPTER 7

# Inchoate Crimes

*Advocacy: Making a Closing Argument*

**LESTER NYGAARD AND ED BLUMQUIST** are being tried for conspiracy and attempted armed robbery. You are preparing for your closing statement and reviewing the trial record:

## ▶ Trial Record

### Opening Statements

During opening statement, the prosecutor said that Lester was in dire financial straits. As a result, he and Ed, Lester's cousin, decided to rob the Pilot gas station and convenience store on the main highway. The prosecutor further said that Lester borrowed a Ruger American hunting rifle and then drove to the Pilot where he parked. Apparently, Lester fell asleep in the car outside the store with the gun in his lap. Officer Raylan Givens saw the gun in Lester's lap when he walked by the car on his way to get a doughnut. He then arrested Lester for having an unregistered firearm. (The unregistered firearm charge was subsequently dismissed.) Ed and Lester were charged with conspiracy and attempted armed robbery.

The defense waived opening argument.

### ❱ Trial Proof

During trial, the witnesses have testified as follows:

#### For the Prosecution

**Officer Givens** testified that when he stopped to "refuel" at Pilot, he walked by a green Buick Skylark and saw a man, apparently asleep, in the driver's seat with a rifle in his lap. Givens drew his weapon and banged on the door of the car. When the individual looked up, Givens ordered him to raise his hands and "stay completely still." Officer Givens then opened the door and, while keeping his weapon focused on the driver, reached in and grabbed the rifle. He then ordered the driver out of the car, and ordered him to face the vehicle and put his hands on the roof. Once the individual complied, Officer Givens then took the person's wallet and identified him as Lester Nygaard. Mr. Nygaard readily conceded his identity.

Givens then asked for registration for the rifle from Nygaard, who responded that "he didn't have it, he borrowed it from his cousin, Ed." Givens then arrested Lester for possessing an unregistered firearm.

Givens later interviewed Ed Blumquist and his wife, Peggy. Ed said he didn't know Lester had borrowed the gun. Ed then said "and that's all I know or will say." Givens then interviewed Peggy separately.

**Peggy Blumquist,** was called as a witness by the prosecution. She testified that she saw Ed and Lester talking for an hour or two before Lester was arrested, when she and Ed were visiting him. Peggy admitted that she heard Lester say "okay, let's knock over the Pilot." She never heard Ed say anything, but noted "he is kind of quiet." Finally, she admitted she saw him nod in response to Lester.

Peggy also testified that Lester and his wife, Pearl, were in dire financial straits and were facing eviction. She described Lester as "desper-
ate." When presented with a note by the prosecutor,
Peggy said it looked "very much like the note" that Lester put on the
table when he left the house that day. She also admitted that Ed's
hunting rifle was in a rack in the cab of their pickup truck
parked outside at the time and that she hasn't seen it since. During
cross-examination, Peggy said Lester never said anything when he
left, and she never saw him with a gun. She also could not remember
if the rifle was missing from the cab of the pickup truck when they left
Lester's house.

The note, admitted into evidence, is copied here.

Pearl

Gone to take care of our

$$ problems!!!

     Back real soon.

          L

## For the Defense

*Pearl Nygaard was the only defense witness. She testified that Lester loved to hunt. He also used to regularly go to the shooting range to practice. But he had recently had to pawn his hunting rifle because they needed money so badly. She also testified that Lester had told her the morning before he was arrested that he "might have a line on a job." On cross-examination, she admitted that she was at the grocery store when Ed and Peggy stopped by the Nygaard house. When she returned Lester was gone. She also admitted seeing the note on the kitchen counter.*

## ▶ Jury Instructions

The judge has informed the prosecution and defense that she will give the following instructions to the jury before deliberations, in addition to standard preliminary instructions about the role of the jury.

### Burden of Proof

The law presumes that a defendant is innocent of the charge[s] against [him] [her]. This presumption remains with the defendant throughout every stage of the trial, and it is not overcome unless from all the evidence in the case you are convinced beyond a reasonable doubt that the defendant is guilty.

The state has the burden of proving the guilt of the defendant beyond a reasonable doubt, and this burden never shifts but remains on the state throughout the trial of the case. The defendant is not required to prove [his] [her] innocence. The state must have proven beyond a reasonable doubt all of the elements of the crime charged.

Reasonable doubt is that doubt engendered by an investigation of all the proof in the case and an inability, after such investigation, to let the mind rest easily as to the certainty of guilt. Reasonable doubt does not mean a doubt that may arise from possibility. Absolute certainty of guilt is not demanded by the law to convict of any criminal charge, but moral certainty is required, and this certainty is required as to every proposition of proof requisite to constitute the offense.

## Conspiracy

Any person who conspires to commit an offense is guilty of a crime.

For you to find a defendant guilty of criminal conspiracy, the state must have proven beyond a reasonable doubt the existence of the following essential elements:

1.  that the defendant entered into an agreement with one (1) or more people to commit the offense of armed robbery. It is not necessary that the object of the agreement be attained; and

2.  that each of the parties to the conspiracy had the intent to commit the offense of armed robbery; and

3.  that each party acting for the purpose of promoting or facilitating the commission of the offense of armed robbery agreed that one or more of them would engage in conduct which constitutes the offense of armed robbery; and

4.  that one (1) of the parties to the conspiracy committed an overt act in furtherance of the conspiracy. An overt act is an act done by one of the parties to carry out the intent of the conspiracy, and it must be a step toward the execution of the conspiracy.

## Attempt

Any person who attempts to commit a criminal offense is guilty of a crime.

For you to find a person guilty of criminal attempt, the state must have proven beyond a reasonable doubt the existence of the following essential elements:

1.  that the defendant intended to commit the specific offense of *armed robbery*;

2.  that the defendant did some act intending to complete a course of action or cause a result that would constitute armed robbery under the circumstances, as the defendant believed them to be at the time, and [his] [her] actions constituted a substantial step toward the commission of *armed robbery*. The defendant's actions do not constitute a substantial step unless the defendant's entire course of action clearly shows [his] [her] intent to commit *armed robbery*

The essential elements necessary to constitute *armed robbery* are as follows:

## Armed Robbery

Any person who commits the offense of *armed robbery* is guilty of a crime.

For you to find a defendant guilty of this offense, the state must have proven beyond a reasonable doubt the existence of the following essential elements:

1.   that the defendant knowingly obtained or exercised control over property owned by Pilot ; and

2.   that the defendant did not have the owner's effective consent; and

3.   that the defendant intended to deprive the owner of the property; and

4.   that the defendant took such property from the person of another by the use of violence or by putting the person in fear; and

5.   that the defendant took such property intentionally or knowingly.

6.   that the defendant accomplished this act with a deadly weapon or by display of any article used or fashioned to lead the alleged victim to reasonably believe it to be a deadly weapon;

The fear constituting an element of robbery is fear of present personal peril from violence offered or impending. Resistance of the party robbed is not required.

The taking from the person may be actual or constructive: it is actual when the taking is immediately from the person, and constructive when in the possession of the person or in the person's presence.

## ❯ Exercise

You represent either the State, Lester Nygaard, or Ed Blumquist, as assigned by your professor. Prepare a five to seven minute closing argument on behalf of your client based on the trial proof and guided by the instructions that will be given by the judge after closing arguments.

 ## Points to Consider

1. **The Elements.** List each crime and the elements that have to be proven to help you organize your closing. What is the proof on each of the elements? Where is the proof missing or weak, if at all? Has the state's burden of reasonable proof been met and how?

2. **Persuading the Jury.** The purpose of closing is to try to persuade the jury about the overall significance of the proof as applied to the law. Closing arguments are the opportunity for each party to remind jurors about key testimony or evidence presented and to persuade them to adopt an interpretation favorable to the party's position. Lawyers are free to use hypothetical analogies to make their points, to comment on the credibility of the witnesses, to discuss how they believe the various pieces of the puzzle fit into a compelling whole, and to advocate why jurors should decide the case in the client's or state's favor.

3. **Order of Closing Arguments.** Because the prosecution bears the
   burden of proof, the prosecution presents closing argument first.
   The prosecution also usually has a chance to do a rebuttal closing
   after the defense. You may want to think about and try to anticipate
   what opposing counsel will argue and respond to those arguments
   as part of your closing.

4. **Taking the Fifth.** Because of the privilege against self-incrimina-
   tion derived from the fifth amendment, neither Lester nor Ed had to
   testify at trial. In addition, to protect that privilege the prosecution
   is not permitted to comment on that failure to testify during
   closing argument.

## Closing Argument Outline

**Notes for Closing**

1. Key Exhibits

2. Key Testimony

3: Instructions (key language to review with the jury)

4. Major Themes

**Closing Outline**

A. Introduction

B.

C.

D.

E. Conclusion

# CHAPTER 8

## Sexting, Sentencing and Collateral Consequences
### *Drafting a Sentencing Memorandum*

**YOU ARE A** law clerk working for a local trial court judge, Donna Emery. She asks you to draft a sentencing memorandum for a high-profile sexting case involving Blake Williams, the 18-year-old son of state senator, Charles Williams. Blake was charged with (1) unlawful photography in violation of privacy and (2) sexual exploitation of a minor. The charging affidavit reads:

---

### *CRIMINAL COURT AFFIDAVIT OF COMPLAINT*

The affiant, Officer Tim Price (Identification Badge No. 5435), after first being duly sworn according to law, states that a criminal offense has been committed in this county, by the defendant, **BLAKE JAMES WILLIAMS**, whose last known address is 75 Willow Road.

Further, the affiant swears that the essential facts constituting the said offense and the sources of the affiant's information are as follows:

Blake Williams, a white male, sexually exploited and unlawfully photographed Vanessa Martin, age 17, in violation of §§ 39–17–1003 and 39–17–1004, respectively. Williams asked Martin via text to send him a picture to "get him through the night." About ten minutes later, Martin sent three photographs by text to Williams. The photographs depicted Martin in different stages of removing her clothing. In the last picture, Martin is

---

97

standing in front of a mirror naked. About thirty minutes later, Williams texted, "You are so beautiful. Thank you." Days after the picture transmission, Martin's mother found the pictures on the family's shared iCloud account and realized the pictures were in every family member's digital photo album. After confronting her daughter and learning about Williams' text prompting the pictures, Martin's mother called the police. Officer Timothy Price responded to the call, viewed the pictures, and confiscated the phone. When Williams spoke to Officer Price, he admitted receiving Martin's pictures by text. Officer Price confiscated Williams' phone and got a warrant to search it. The search located the pictures that Martin sent and additional obscene pictures of Martin that Williams took with his phone over a month before. The defendant was arrested and then transported to the police station for booking and processing.

Signed:

*Timothy J. Price*
Timothy J. Price

Personally sworn to and subscribed by the affiant before me this day.

It appearing that the offenses of (1) sexual exploitation of a minor, under § 39–17–1003, a Class D felony, and (2) unlawful photography in violation of privacy under § 39–17–1004, a Class A misdemeanor, have been committed by the defendant, and it appearing from said affidavit that there is probable cause that the defendant violated § 39–17–1003 and § 39–17–1004, this judge commands the arrest of the defendant and the defendant's appearance at the next possible court setting.

Signed:

*David Weddington*
Magistrate Judge

**STATE WARRANT:** #273390

Given that Williams' father is a public figure, the press has been relentless about the case. Blake Williams decided to take a plea to violating § 39-17-1004, a class A misdemeanor, for unlawful photography in violation of privacy, and the prosecution agreed to drop the felony charge of sexual exploitation of a minor. Because the defense and prosecution could not agree on the appropriate sentence for Williams, as happens in some cases, both sides presented oral arguments to the judge explaining their sentencing positions. Williams' defense attorney also presented an affidavit from Vanessa Martin, which you have in the file. You also have excerpts from the transcript of this hearing. The attorneys for both sides disagree about two critical aspects of sentencing and raised the following questions for your judge:

1. Should the defendant receive judicial diversion under § 40-35-313? In your jurisdiction, § 40-35-313 authorizes any defendant who "has not previously been convicted of a felony or a Class A misdemeanor" and "who has not been granted judicial diversion or pretrial diversion before," to ask the court to "defer the proceedings without entering a judgment" provided that the defendant "successfully complete a probationary term that can include reasonable conditions, including but not limited to like community service, counseling, or jail time of less than 30 days. If the conditions are met, the "court shall discharge the person and dismiss the proceedings against the person." Once the dismissal is entered, the defendant can petition the court to expunge the public record referring to the proceeding. Should the judge grant Mr. Williams judicial diversion upon successful completion of his sentence?

2. Should the defendant be placed on the sex offender registry? The judge can decide whether or not to order Williams to register as a sex offender under § 39-17-1004(f). The sex offender registry is a publicly accessible database that includes a sexual offender's race,

gender, current photograph, address, phone number, date of birth, social security number, place of employment, any vehicles owned and their license plate numbers, email addresses, social media accounts, and information about the conviction. The sex offender registry's reporting requirements include: regular check-ins with a probation officer, therapy as recommended by an annual sex offender evaluation, restrictions on the proximity of housing and employment to schools and churches, and notification of any changes to a residence or employment. The minimum number of years on the registry is five years. Should the judge place Mr. Williams on the sex offender registry?

Judge Emery will announce Mr. Williams sentence at a court appearance in two weeks. Judge Emery asks you to write a sentencing memorandum that outlines what sentence you recommend and asks you to include the appropriate sentencing range, the mitigating and aggravating factors she should consider, and your rationale for the sentence. The judge will use your sentencing memorandum to determine Williams' sentence.

## ▶ Applicable Statutes

### § 39–17–1003. **Offense of Sexual Exploitation of a Minor.**

a.    It is unlawful for any person to knowingly possess obscene material depicting a minor, or a minor engaged in sexual or simulated sexual activity.

b.    "Obscene" means that the average person applying contemporary community standards, would find that the work, taken as a whole, appeals to the prurient interest; and that the work, taken as a whole, lacks serious literary, artistic, political, or scientific value.

c.    A violation of this section is a Class D felony, punishable by 2 to 4 years incarceration, a fine of up to $5000, and registration as a sexual offender.

### § 39–17–1004. Unlawful Photography in Violation of Privacy.

a.    It is an offense for a person to knowingly photograph another, when the individual is in a place where there is a reasonable expectation of privacy, without the prior effective consent of the individual, or in the case of a minor, without the prior effective consent of the minor's parent or guardian, if the photograph:

    1.    Would offend or embarrass an ordinary person if such person appeared in the photograph; and

    2.    Was taken for the purpose of sexual arousal or gratification of the defendant.

b.    As used in this section, unless the context otherwise requires, "photograph" means any photograph, still or moving, or any videotape or live television transmission of any individual so that the individual is readily identifiable.

c.    All photographs taken in violation of this section shall be confiscated and, after their use as evidence, destroyed.

d.    A violation of this section is a Class A misdemeanor, punishable by up to 11 months and 29 days incarceration plus a fine of up to $500.

e.    If the photography is disseminated in any way, a violation of this section is a Class E felony, punishable by up to 2 years incarceration plus a fine of up to $2500.

f.    The trial judge may order, after taking into account the facts and circumstances surrounding the offense, including the offense for which the person was originally charged and whether the conviction was the result of a plea bargain agreement, that the person be required to register as a sexual offender.

## ▶  Sentencing Documents

To help you prepare a sentencing memorandum, you are provided with the following: (1) excerpts from the transcript of the last court appearance which include the prosecutor's sentencing recommendation and the defense attorney's response, (2) Vanessa Martin's affidavit, and (3) the relevant sentencing statutes.

### 1. Transcribed Excerpt from Prosecutor's Argument

*Although the prosecution could have proved its cases for both charges, Your Honor, the state offered to drop the felony charge given Mr. Williams' acceptance of responsibility for his actions. He immediately admitted to receiving the text messages sent by Ms. Martin, taking obscene pictures of Ms. Martin in his bedroom only one month prior, and sending one of the pictures to a friend, a crime we chose not to charge him with. He assisted the prosecution in getting the illicit picture of Ms. Martin out of circulation by giving us his friend's address and phone.*

*Although the A misdemeanor that he is pleading to exposes him to a jail sentence of 11 months and 29 days, I recommend that this Court be lenient given his age and the fact that this is his first offense. Although Vanessa Martin wants the court to believe that she acted of her own volition, she, unlike Mr. Williams, was a minor at the time.*

*Most importantly, the state asks the Court to use this case to send a clear message to teenagers throughout this jurisdiction that texting or emailing obscene pictures is a crime. To that end, the state recommends that the Court order three things as a part of Mr. Williams' sentence. First, the Court should order Mr. Williams to serve a 15-day jail sentence. Second, upon release from jail, the Court should order Mr. Williams to attend and successfully complete weekly sex offender therapy sessions for 10 months. Third, the state requests that the Court order Mr. Williams to register as a sex offender, which is authorized by § 39-17-1004(f), until he is found to no longer be a risk to society. If Mr. Williams performs well and abides by the registry's requirements, he can file a request for termination of the sex offender registration requirements in five years.*

### 2. Transcribed Excerpt from Defense Counsel's Argument

*Mr. Williams is deeply sorry for the embarrassment and harm that he has caused Ms. Martin whom he fell in love with 6 months ago. He did not have any idea that the pictures he took or received would have caused her this harm. He even offered unsolicited information to the prosecutor about sending his friend one of the pictures so that the police could permanently delete it from his friend's phone. But he now knows that he should have been more aware of the embarrassment that taking these pictures would cause Ms. Martin and her family. He is very sorry for his mistake.*

*Mr. Williams, however, is also just a young man himself. Although he is 18 years old, which brings him under adult court jurisdiction, he is barely an adult. He is a senior at Preston Academy, maintains good grades, and has a bright future ahead of him. For the past three years, he has been the star forward on Preston Academy's Varsity Basketball team. He hopes to play college basketball and major in business. He* also regularly attends the United Methodist Church on Broadway with his parents. The pastor of his church and his basketball coach are here today to show their support. They are sitting with his father, Senator Williams, his mother, Deborah Williams, his maternal grandparents, and his older sister, Charlotte, who is a nurse at Baptist Hospital.

We ask that the court take into account Mr. Williams' age and his relationship with Ms. Martin when determining his sentence in light of this generation's culture of texting. Your Honor, it is so very different from when we grew up. Teens have adopted a language about sending "nudes" or "nude selfies." Although the exact prevalence of "sexting" by teens is unknown, in one study published in Cyberpsychology, Behavior and Social Networking, researchers surveyed 1,000 students in the 10th grade and found that 25% of the boys and 32% of the girls had taken at least one nude picture and sent it to someone.

Given these mitigating circumstances, jail would be an extremely harsh punishment for Mr. Williams. Instead, we ask this court to order Mr. Williams to go to therapy for these incidents and to place him on probation for 10 months.

Most importantly, Your Honor, Mr. Williams is not the type of child predator contemplated by the Sex Offender Registry. Mr. Williams asks that the Court, after weighing all the facts and considering a totality of the circumstances in this case, exercise its discretion and not place Mr. Williams on the sex offender registry.

Finally, we seek a grant of judicial diversion in this case. Because Mr. Williams is a first offender, and § 39-17-1004 is not a mandatory sex offense, he is eligible for judicial diversion under § 40-35-313. Judicial diversion requires Mr. Williams to enter a guilty plea at this time, but ultimately if he successfully completes the terms of his sentence, his case will be dismissed, and it can ultimately be expunged. If he does *not succeed, the conviction remains on his record for life. But diversion will give him a second chance, as the statute intends, to live a life as a productive and engaged citizen.*

### 1. **Vanessa Martin's Affidavit**

*My name is Vanessa Martin, and I am 17 years old. I am a junior at Preston Academy, a co-ed private school. I am a good student, a cheerleader, and a class representative on the Student Council. I also play on the varsity volleyball team.*

*I had been dating Blake Williams for over 6 months when this unfortunate incident happened. I have known Blake since I moved to our neighborhood when I was in the 5th grade. Since the incident, though, my mother demanded that I end my relationship with Blake. But I still care about him a great deal. I took the pictures I sent voluntarily without being coerced by Blake. I wanted to surprise him and had no intention for anyone else to see them. Because this case has been in the news, it has embarrassed me, and I have lost many friends. I even asked the prosecutor to drop the charges. I know that I did not act with good judgment, and I hope that you will take my role into account. I feel like Blake is being punished for both of our actions.*

## ▶ Relevant Sentencing Statutes

### § 40–35–113. **Mitigating Factors.**

If appropriate for the offense, mitigating factors may include, but are not limited to:

1. The defendant's criminal conduct neither caused nor threatened serious bodily injury;

2.   The defendant acted under strong provocation;

3.   Substantial grounds exist tending to excuse or justify the defendant's criminal conduct, though failing to establish a defense;

4.   The defendant played a minor role in the commission of the offense;

5.   Before detection, the defendant compensated or made a good faith attempt to compensate the victim of criminal conduct for the damage or injury the victim sustained;

6.   The defendant, because of youth or old age, lacked substantial judgment in committing the offense;

7.   The defendant was motivated by a desire to provide necessities for the defendant's family or the defendant's self;

8.   The defendant was suffering from a mental or physical condition that significantly reduced the defendant's culpability for the offense;

9.   The defendant assisted the authorities in uncovering offenses committed by other persons or in locating or recovering any property or person involved in the crime;

10.   The defendant, although guilty of the crime, committed the offense under such unusual circumstances that it is unlikely that a sustained intent to violate the law motivated the criminal conduct;

11.   The defendant took responsibility for the crime and admitted to his wrongful conduct;

12.   The defendant acted under duress or under the domination of another person; or

13.   Any other factor consistent with the purposes of this chapter.

### § 40–35–114. Enhancement Factors.

If appropriate for the offense and if not already an essential element of the offense, the court shall consider, but is not bound by, the following advisory factors in determining whether to enhance a defendant's sentence:

1.   The defendant has a previous history of criminal convictions or criminal behavior, in addition to those necessary to establish the appropriate range;

2.   The offense involved more than one victim or a victim that was a minor;

3.   A victim of the offense was particularly vulnerable because of age or physical or mental disability;

4.   The personal injuries inflicted upon, or the amount of damage to property sustained by or taken from, the victim was particularly great;

5.   The offense involved a victim and was committed to gratify the defendant's desire for pleasure or excitement;

6.   The defendant, before trial or sentencing, failed to comply with the conditions of a sentence involving release into the community;

7.   The defendant possessed or employed a firearm, explosive device, or other deadly weapon during the commission of the offense;

8.   During the commission of the crime, the defendant intentionally inflicted serious bodily injury upon another person, or the actions of the defendant resulted in the death of, or serious bodily injury to, a victim or a person other than the intended victim;

9.   The defendant was adjudicated to have committed a delinquent act or acts as a juvenile that would constitute a felony if committed by an adult; or

10.   The offense was an act of terrorism, or was related to an act of terrorism.

▶ **Exercise**

Prepare a sentencing memorandum for your judge, using the statutes and documents above, that states the criminal sentence that you would impose and what facts and law support your sentencing decision. Address whether or not: (a) diversion should be granted under § 40–35–315, and (b) registration with the sex offender registry should be ordered under § 39–17–1004(f).

## Points to Consider

1. **The Law.** The only mens rea required by this statute is that Mr. Williams had *knowledge* that he is in possession a nude photo of a minor. What do you think about this culpability requirement? Do you think the statute was intended for a defendant like Mr. Williams?

2. **The Plea.** Under § 40–35–113(11), taking a plea—admitting to guilt and taking responsibility for the crime—is a mitigating factor that can help reduce a sentence. Could making a plea a mitigating factor for a sentence reduction induce a defendant to take a plea?

3. **Facts.** What facts matter in your sentencing decision and how do the sentencing options account for them?

4. **Sentencing Range.** Outline the sentencing range that the judge must consider. What is the most punitive sentence that can be imposed? What is the least punitive sentence that can be imposed? How does judicial diversion under § 40–35–313 fit into this range?

5. **Mitigating and Aggravating Factors under §40–35–113 and § 40–35–114.** What mitigating factors apply to Williams' case? Do any aggravating factors apply? Are there factors that you want the judge to consider that are missing from these two lists? Decide how these factors will influence your recommendation and be sure to explain them in your sentencing memo.

6. **Collateral Consequences of a Conviction.** A conviction resulting from a guilty plea in this case will create a permanent criminal record for Mr. Williams. Even after a criminal sentence is complete, a conviction, is available in most states through online public databases. Every background check by an employer, educational institution, or landlord will reveal Williams' conviction making it more difficult for him to obtain a job, professional license, college degree, or housing. Are you worried about these consequences?

7. **The Sex Offender Registry.** As explained above, the statute that Williams is pleading to, § 39–17–1004, can trigger the specific collateral consequence of the sex offender registry. A discretionary statute for the registry is actually unusual because most sex offense statutes make the registry automatic. Should the judge order Mr. Williams to register as a sex offender? Why or why not?

8. **Theories of Punishment.** The purpose of criminal law is to determine the appropriate level of punishment for each individual defendant. Think back to the earlier discussion of punishment theories including retribution, deterrence, and rehabilitation. What punishment theory or theories will guide your sentencing recommendation? Do you agree with the prosecution that the judge should punish Mr. Williams harshly to deter other teens from sharing obscene images by text? Or do you support a more rehabilitative approach that takes into account his age and ability to change as his matures into adulthood?

## Sentencing Memorandum

### State v. Williams

A.   Discuss the potential sentencing range:

B.   Discuss mitigating and aggravating factors:

C.   Recommend a sentence for Williams and explain your decision. (Address whether Williams should be granted diversion under § 40-35-313.)

D.   Discuss whether the judge should mandate that Williams be placed on the sex offender registry.

# CHAPTER 9

## Defenses

### *Counseling and Negotiation*
### *Re: Potential Plea Agreement*

**THE CONTENTS OF** the relevant case file are as follows:

---

**Rocky Top Sheriff's Department**

**Investigative Report**

**Detective:** H. Bosch
**Date:** May 31

Responded to call at 6429 Kiffen Drive. Uniformed officers had already secured the crime scene.

Investigation revealed that the homeowner, James McGill, was at home with his girlfriend, Kim Wexler, his father and his two children, when his motion sensors began going off and his dogs began barking about 1 a.m. The light and the barking woke McGill up. McGill stated that he then woke Wexler before getting his father's loaded shotgun to make sure his shed, where he kept rare car parts, was secured.

McGill said that as he approached the shed, he bent down and saw what he thought were feet. He stated that then a person came through a gap in the fence right at McGill. McGill said he was "scared to death." As the person came through the fence, McGill began screaming and fired his shotgun "at least twice."

Specifically, Mr. McGill gave the following statement: "He scared me to death. I was holding the shotgun out in front of me for mine and my girlfriend's safety. I got

---

low, leaned in, and looked. I wasn't sure, but I thought I saw some feet. Then he came right at me, I screamed like a child and fired the shotgun. After I realized what had happened, I called 911."

Ms. Wexler confirmed Mr. McGill's version of the events, though she stayed just inside the back door, a position approximately 110 feet from the shooting site. The site of the shooting was at the edge of the McGill property near an old fence and next two a locked shed.

The victim, identified as Tuco Salamanca, died at the scene. Salamanca, 21, had two misdemeanor drug convictions.

Further investigation ongoing.

---

### OFFICE OF THE COUNTY CORONER

| **DATE and HOUR AUTOPSY PERFORMED:**<br>6/1, 8:30 a.m. by<br>Darinka Polchan, M.D.<br>555 Jackson Avenue<br>Rocky Top 38655<br>662-234-XXXX | **Assistant:**<br>Victoria Witt, M.D.<br><br>**Full Autopsy Performed** |
|---|---|

#### SUMMARY PRELIMINARY REPORT OF AUTOPSY

| **Name:**<br>SALAMANCA, Tuco | **Coroner's Case #:**<br>2013-129 |
|---|---|
| **Date of Birth:** 06/23 | **Age:** 21 |
| **Race:** Hispanic | **Sex:** Male |
| **Date of Death:** 5/31 | **Body Identified by:**<br>Karla Salamanca, mother |
| **Case #**<br>003511-04K-2013 | **Investigative Agency:**<br>Rocky Top Sheriff's Department |

**EVIDENCE OF TREATMENT**

    N/A

**EXTERNAL EXAMINATION**

The autopsy is begun at 8:30. The body is presented in a black body bag. At the time of examination, the body is wrapped in a clear, plastic tarp.

The body is that of a normally developed, well-nourished male measuring 71 inches in length, weighing 175 pounds, and appearing generally consistent with the stated age of 21 years.

The body is cold with slowly declining rigor. Pronounced lividity is present on the lateral posterior of the body in the regions of the heels, legs, back, arms and is pinkish in color. Purplish lividity is also present on the posterior of the neck.

The scalp is covered by short, blonde hair, averaging 2 inches in length. The skull is symmetric. The eyes are open and the irises appear to be brown. Pupils are asymmetrically dilated and slightly cloudy. The teeth are natural and well maintained.

### DESCRIPTION OF INJURIES—SUMMARY

(1) The anterior chest has large wound approximately 9 cm in diameter approximately four cm left of center. Wound is consistent with close range shotgun discharge. Depth of wound is 3 cm.

**Opinion:** This is a fatal injury though death not immediate.

(2) Portion of upper right shoulder muscle missing again from apparent shotgun blast with large wound surrounding area.

**Opinion:** This is a non-fatal injury

(3) Large 12 cm diameter wound on lower back from similar cause. Depth 5 cm.

**Opinion:** This is a fatal injury though death not immediate.

Pellets removed from all three wounds.

Overall, most of the wounds suggest a close range shooting from shot gun.

### LABORATORY DATA

**Drug Screen Results:**

| | | |
|------|------|------|
| *BLOOD* | *ETHANOL* | *NEG* |
| *BLOOD* | *CANNABINOIDS-ETS* | *POS* |
| *BLOOD* | *COCAINE-ETS* | *NEG* |
| *BLOOD* | *OPIATES-ETS* | *NEG* |
| *BLOOD* | *AMPHETAMINE-ETS* | *NEG* |

### OPINION

**Time of Death:** Body temperature and rigor and livor mortis approximate the time of death between 2:00 am and 2:15 am on May 31.

**Immediate Cause of Death:** Exsanguination due to gunshot wounds.

**Manner of Death:** Homicide

**Rocky Top Sheriff's Department**

Investigative Report Update

**Detective: H. Bosch**

**Date: June 3**

Received call from Steve Scott, Bureau of Investigation, firearms division. Scott examined body of Salamanca. Scott's opinion is that shot to Salamanca's chest and shoulder from 2 feet away. Back wound from 3 feet.

▶ MEMORANDUM
**Attorney Work Product**

**To: File**
**From: You**
**Re: McGill Case—Client Interview**

Met with James "Jimmy" McGill today. He is a 40 year old white male. McGill is out on bond on second-degree murder charges. Reviewed the investigative reports and McGill confirmed accuracy of reports. Added that there had been reports of three burglaries in the neighborhood over the past six months.

He has owned the shotgun for over twenty years. He used to hunt in his 20's, but has not done so for years. He stores the shotgun in the utility room off the kitchen. He has lived on Kiffen Drive for twelve years and likes the neighborhood. It is suburban rural with slightly bigger lots than closer to town. He has a garden.

He also collects and sells rare car parts as a side business. His main employment is selling insurance. He estimates that he has over $30,000 worth of parts in his shed at any one time.

I explained the charges. We talked about the pre-trial and trial process. I explained the proof to date. We also discussed the viability of self-defense as a defense. I explained the Rocky Top statute.

I promised to keep him informed of any activity on the case.

## ▶ Potentially Applicable Statutes

### § 39–13–203. Second Degree Murder.

Second degree murder is a knowing killing of another.

### § 39–13–204. Voluntary Manslaughter.

Voluntary manslaughter is the intentional or knowing killing of another in a state of passion produced by adequate provocation sufficient to lead a reasonable person to act in an irrational manner.

### § 39–13–205. Involuntary Manslaughter.

Involuntary manslaughter is the reckless killing of another.

### § 39–13–206. Criminally Negligent Homicide.

Criminally negligent homicide is criminally negligent conduct that results in death.

### § 39–11–401. Self-Defense.

a.   As used in this section, unless the context otherwise requires:

1. "Business" means a commercial enterprise or establishment owned by a person as all or part of the person's livelihood or is under the owner's control or who is an employee or agent of the owner with responsibility for protecting persons and property and shall include the interior and exterior premises of the business;

2. "Curtilage" means the area surrounding a dwelling that is necessary, convenient and habitually used for family purposes and for those activities associated with the sanctity of a person's home;

3. "Dwelling" means a building or conveyance of any kind, including any attached porch, whether the building or conveyance is temporary or permanent, mobile or immobile, that has a roof over it, including a tent, and is designed for or capable of use by people;

4. "Residence" means a dwelling in which a person resides, either temporarily or permanently, or is visiting as an invited guest, or any dwelling, building or other appurtenance within the curtilage of the residence; and

5. "Vehicle" means any motorized vehicle that is self-propelled and designed for use on public highways to transport people or property.

b. A person who is not engaged in unlawful activity and is in a place where the person has a right to be has no duty to retreat before threatening or using force against another person when and to the degree the person reasonably believes the force is immediately necessary to protect against the other's use or attempted use of unlawful force.

c. A person who is not engaged in unlawful activity and is in a place where the person has a right to be has no duty to retreat before threatening or using force intended or likely to cause death or serious bodily injury, if:

1. The person has a reasonable belief that there is an imminent danger of death or serious bodily injury;

2. The danger creating the belief of imminent death or serious bodily injury is real, or honestly believed to be real at the time; and

3. The belief of danger is founded upon reasonable grounds.

d. Any person using force intended or likely to cause death or serious bodily injury within a residence, business, dwelling or vehicle is presumed to have held a reasonable belief of imminent death or serious bodily injury to self, family, a member of the household or a person visiting as an invited guest, when that force is used against another person, who unlawfully and forcibly enters or has unlawfully and forcibly entered the residence, business, dwelling or vehicle, and the person using defensive force knew or had reason to believe that an unlawful and forcible entry occurred.

# Office of the Rocky Top
# District Attorney General

200 Main Street

Rocky Top

You
Attorney at Law
410 Main Street, Suite 400
Rocky Top
        Re: State vs. McGill

Dear You:

I have carefully reviewed the file and considered our previous phone conversation. While I understand that Mr. McGill's situation is a bit unique, the simple truth is that criminal trespass does not justify a death. The mere fact that Mr. Salamanca was on your client's property did not give Mr. McGill the right to shoot him.

However, in light of the unique aspects of this case, the state is willing to offer Mr. McGill a sentence of ten years in return for a guilty plea on the second degree murder charge. As you know, the normal sentencing range for the charge is 15 to 45 years. I believe, however, that Judge Haller will approve this plea agreement.

I look forward to your response and your client's agreement. As you know, I am not generally receptive to protracted plea negotiations. If your client is unwilling to accept a reasonable plea offer, at trial we will seek a sentence in the middle of the sentencing range.

Sincerely,

Jim

James Trotter
Assistant District Attorney

### ▶ Exercise

1. Meet with your client to counsel him regarding the plea offer.

2. Based on your client counseling meeting, draft a response to the plea offer.

 Points to Consider:

1. **Self Defense.** How applicable is the defense? Who has to prove the elements of the defense? What facts support application of the defense? Is the presumption of justified action under the statute applicable here? What is the relationship, if any, between facts supporting the defense and proof regarding you client's mental state?

2. **Negotiation Strategy.** Is it advisable to negotiate further on a possible plea? What are the facts that are advantageous for your client? Disadvantageous? What approach should you take? Do you make a counteroffer? Would that be your final offer? How much support for any alternative proposal do you need to provide? Why or why not?

3. **Decision-Making Authority.** Who has the authority to decide whether to accept or reject the plea offer? Does it have to be communicated to the client? If the plea is not accepted, who decides what the counteroffer should be? What are the respective roles of the client and the lawyer in making decisions in a plea negotiation?

# Client Counseling Outline

Attorney Name:

Client:

Date:

Client Goals:

Client Concerns:

Key Discussion Points:

Detail of Plea Offer:

Pros:

Cons:

Recommendation:

Decision:

# Negotiation Plan

1. Details of plea offer

2. Problems with offer

    A. Legal authority and analysis

    B. Non-legal considerations

3. Analysis of state's position

    A. Probable reasoning

    B. Probable bottom line

4. Likely outcome without agreement

5. Counter proposal and reasoning

6. Client's bottom line

## Response to Plea Offer

James Trotter, Esq.
Assistant District Attorney
Office of the District Attorney General
200 Main Street
Rocky Top

      Re: State v. McGill

Dear Attorney-General Trotter:

Sincerely,

# CHAPTER 10

# Accomplice Liability
### *Negotiating a Plea*

**IN COURT,** your supervising attorney hands you a new case. Twenty-year-old Calvin Jones was arrested with two co-defendants around 8:30 a.m. on Saturday morning. You look at the charges: aggravated burglary, criminal responsibility for the conduct of another, and facilitation of a felony. The criminal warrant alleges:

Around 6:30 a.m. on Saturday morning, the defendant, Calvin Jones along with his co-defendants, Alex Young and James Smith, burglarized a residence at 7425 Lawford Road. Earlier that evening, co-defendant Smith, who was in possession of a gun, suggested that they go to the home of the victim, known to Defendant Smith, and steal items of value including jewelry. While co-defendants Smith and Young entered the residence, the defendant remained in the vehicle with Defendant Young's car keys to serve as a lookout.

Leaving the scene at around 7:45 a.m., Defendant Young was driving his black SUV 50 miles an hour in a 40 mile an hour

speed zone. When Officer Hitchens pulled over the car, Young and Smith were in the front and two women and the defendant were in the second row of the vehicle. Officer Hitchens, approaching the vehicle on the passenger's side for his safety, saw a silver metal object that appeared to be a gun on the floor below the glove box. Calling for backup, he ordered each passenger out of the vehicle with their hands behind their heads. Upon searching the vehicle, Officer Hitchens found a gun, a jewelry box, and an unopened lockbox. He arrested the defendant and his co-defendants, and took all three down to the station for booking.

The judge arraigned Calvin Jones on the charges and set the case for a preliminary hearing in three weeks. You agree to meet with opposing counsel prior to the hearing to try and work out a plea deal. You immediately begin to investigate the case to prepare for the negotiation.

Your Jones Case File has the following: (1) Officer Hitchen's summary of Cassandra's statement to him when he stopped the car[1]—this statement informed the officer's decision to charge the three defendants with aggravated burglary. (2) An investigation memo—your investigator has been hard at work gathering the evidence inventory, 911 call, burglary victim's statement, and the investigating detective's log. You also asked your law clerk to pull the relevant statutes, summarize applicable cases, and pull the statute for accessory after the fact, which is not charged in the warrant but is another accomplice liability statute.

---

1   If you are assigned as a prosecutor in this case, Police Officer Hitchens gave you his summary of Cassandra's statement to him at the scene. In an attempt to speed up the negotiation in this case, you provide that statement to defense counsel as early discovery and potential Brady material. Brady material is any evidence that the prosecution has that may be exculpatory to the defense.

## ▶ Jones' Case File

### 1. Officer Hitchen's Summary of Cassandra Young Statement

*Cassandra is 20 years old and goes to Pellissippi State Community College, as do all of the occupants of the car. She is Alex Young's twin sister. She is really mad about what happened. She does not think Calvin or her brother should have been arrested, only James. She said that it was all James' idea.*

*She explained that she was at West Town Mall with her friend, Danielle Rodriguez. Danielle is Calvin's girlfriend—Calvin and Danielle met about 9 months ago and have been dating since. Alex, Calvin, and James have all been close friends since elementary school. James is a junior at Pellissippi State. All five of them hang out together all the time. They still live with their parents to save on rent.*

*The night before the burglary, Cassandra and Danielle were hanging out at the mall until around 10:00 p.m. Alex and James came to pick them up in Alex's black SUV. They had a few beers in the parking lot of the mall and then went to get Calvin who was at work. He works for Dick's Sporting Goods. They picked up Calvin, got burgers and shakes at Cook Out, and then smoked a joint in the parking lot.*

*They were all hanging out, and she admits they smoked marijuana a few times during the night. "Not really a lot," she said. But she also wasn't totally sure how many times or how much marijuana they smoked.*

*Cassandra described going to a bar, The Muse, on Central Avenue. Cassandra said that they got there around 11:30 p.m. and then stayed until probably 1 a.m. It was after last call when they left. She admits to having about four beers and some shots there.*

*Then Alex got a text about a frat party on campus so they drove
there. They were all drinking and smoking at the party. She said that
she hooked up with James and that "he started to be a real jerk to her
though, and I had to push him off of me." She added that they have
dated off and on for the past 2 years.*

*The party was breaking up around 4 a.m. so they all got in the car and
crashed in the football stadium parking lot. Alex didn't seem like he
could drive them home yet. He was pretty wasted and the drive was
about 30 minutes. They ended up sleeping in the car for a few hours.
"We probably slept until 6:30 a.m.," she said.*

*When she woke up, James and Alex were talking, and the car was
parked in a residential neighborhood in front of a white house with a
fence. It was dark. She said that she never went into the house to rob
someone. That was all James' idea. James said that the house belonged
to the Fergusons, who were friends of his parents. They were away for
the weekend, and James' parents were watching their house and taking
care of their cat. James wanted to crash there earlier in the night. He
also told them all that the family had expensive stuff like jewelry and
guns—the family was loaded. She said that Danielle freaked out and
said she wanted to go home. Alex seemed into the idea of not sleeping
in the car and checking out the house to sleep there. Calvin didn't say
anything, but she said that he also didn't say he wanted to go home. He
wanted to keep hanging out. They talked about this for a few minutes
but then decided to go to the frat party instead of the house. She
thought that the issue was over.*

*Her brother noticed she was awake and said that he needed her mace.
So she took it out of her purse and gave it to him. James was pretty ex-
cited, and she saw him put something in his pocket. He always carried a
small handgun around, and he had it out earlier. So she thought that he
brought it inside the house.*

*Cassandra said that it was still dark when they left the car, and it all happened really fast. She said that Calvin and Danielle were asleep at first, but before they left for the house, James woke up Calvin by shaking him. He told Calvin to keep an eye out and watch for anything suspicious. He said, "Get in the front seat. Get in the front. Make sure no one comes—if you see anything at all, call me and we'll get out of there. You hear me. You call me right away. We ain't getting caught in this." He kept yelling for Calvin to wake up. Calvin sat up straight, eyes wide open, and looked around, yelling back, "Okay, Okay. Stop yelling." Alex tossed the keys at Calvin. Calvin opened the door to go in the front seat. Danielle said, "You are not listening to that fool." Calvin sat back down in the back, and passed out again holding the keys. He was half asleep the entire time that Alex and James were gone. He did not seem to know what was happening. At one point, he asked, "Where are those guys?" Then he passed out again.*

*About 20 minutes later, Alex and James came running back carrying stuff. James handed Calvin a jewelry box, and Calvin handed Alex the keys. Danielle was starting to wake up more now and started freaking out and yelling. Calvin said to take him and Danielle home.*

*Alex drove away pretty fast. Cassandra opened the jewelry box and saw a pearl necklace. Calvin shut the box and put it under the passenger's seat. James told Alex to slow down because he was speeding. Then they saw my cruiser and lights behind them.*

*She is willing to sign a statement and testify to all of this, but is not sure what street the house was on. She said that it was a subdivision near where I pulled them over off of Westland.*

*I did find the jewelry box under the passenger's seat, and a gun and the lockbox on the floor of the passengers' seat right by James Smith's legs.*

### 2. Investigation Report Re: Aggravated Burglary Charges

To: You

From: Indira Robinson, Investigator                    PRIVILEGED & CONFIDENTIAL

Re: *7425 Lawford Road, Knoxville, TN*                 ATTORNEY WORK PRODUCT

Five updates:

**(1) Evidence Inventory (#7A54G).**

We just received a copy of the police inventory sheet that lists the contraband recovered from defendant Young's car:

- a 9 mm Beretta Nano. Officer Hitchens sent this out for prints and estimated that we should know of any matches soon. He indicated that he believed it to belong to Young.

- an unopened lockbox that contained $1,080, and

- a jewelry box with:
  - a pearl necklace: estimated at $500
  - a diamond bracelet estimated at $1,400
  - gold earrings: estimated at $60
  - gold necklace: estimated at $150
  - miscellaneous costume jewelry: estimated at $150

**(2) Conversation with Officer Hitchens.**

After we talked, I got Officer Hitchens on the phone. He confirmed that Calvin Jones would not speak with him. He heard Calvin tell all three boys to keep their mouths shut and ask for an attorney. No one besides Cassandra spoke to him about what happened. Cassandra though seemed to have a motive to keep her brother and Calvin out of trouble. He felt like she really pinned it all on James, which felt suspicious to him like she had grudge against him. Danielle, the other girl in the car, was pretty hysterical once I put her in handcuffs and then she asked that I call her father Sergeant Rodriguez from Blount County. As soon as she said who her father was I called him, took her out of the cuffs, and put her in the back of my cruiser. I couldn't help but picture my daughter crying like this in the same situation. She was scared, and it seemed like she wasn't involved at all. She kept repeating that she had asked to go home but that James wouldn't take her. Cassandra's statement confirmed that too. Sergeant Rodriguez got there before I could interview Danielle. Sergeant Rodriguez said that Danielle was a mess, and he handed me his card with his cell number. He said that I could interview Danielle whenever I wanted to. I haven't had a chance to call him yet to I set up an interview with her. I will do that before the hearing. I also asked Officer Hitchens if she seemed drunk or high, and he said that she didn't seem intoxicated. But she did seem scared and upset. He said Cassandra seemed fine too.

I also learned that because Cassandra was the only witness who talked to Officer Hitchens, he wasn't exactly sure what house was burglarized until the Ferguson family came home from vacation on Sunday and reported that their house was broken into.

**(3) 911 call at 3:14 p.m. on the day after the burglary.**

Charles Ferguson identified himself as the caller. He reported that his house at 7425 Lawford Road had been broken into. They returned home that afternoon around 1 p.m. from a vacation in Florida. They noticed that the back basement door was cracked open and the screen was ripped.

**(4) Excerpt from Ms. Ferguson's Statement:**

Detective Janet Moreland responded to the 911 call and interviewed Charles and Janet Ferguson. Here is the relevant part of the statement:

I was going into the backyard to look for our gray cat, Swatch. When I looked near her favorite hiding spot, I noticed that the door to the basement seemed to be open slightly and the screen on the door was torn. Nothing immediately struck us to be missing until I went to my bedroom. Several dresser drawers were removed and dumped. I then noticed my jewelry box was missing. Charles went to his study and noticed our lockbox was gone. The safe had been moved and was on its side. . .

We were away for the week. We went to Florida last Sunday, 7 days ago, and returned today at around 1 p.m. We didn't set our house alarm because our friends from church, the Smiths, needed to get in to feed the cat.

**(5) Detective Moreland's Police Log.**

Detective Moreland wrote in her police log:

> Ms. Ferguson looked particularly shaken up. The jewelry box contained a diamond bracelet that she inherited from her grandmother. I explained that this description seemed to match the contents of a jewelry box that was recovered from three suspects charged with a burglary early Saturday morning. My visual observations of her room and the study were consistent with Ms. Ferguson's statement.
>
> Mr. Ferguson is a pharmacist, and Ms. Ferguson is an elementary school teacher, and they have two teenage boys, Michael and Joseph, who stayed in their rooms playing video games while Detective Moreland investigated the scene.

## ▶ Applicable Statutes

The statutes defining the culpable mental states in this jurisdiction can be found in Chapter Five on pages 63–64.

### § 39–14–400. Definitions for Burglary and Related Offenses.

As used in this part:

a.   Habitation means any structure, including buildings, module units, mobile homes, trailers, and tents, which is designed or adapted for the overnight accommodation of persons, and

b.   Owner means a person in lawful possession of property whether the possession is actual or constructive.

### § 39–14–402. Burglary.

a.   A person commits burglary who, without the effective consent of the property owner, enters a building and commits or attempts to commit a felony, theft or assault;

b.   As used in this section, "enter" means:

1.   Intrusion of any part of the body; or

2.   Intrusion of any object in physical contact with the body or any object controlled by remote control, electronic or otherwise.

c.   Burglary is a Class D felony punishable by up to 10 years in prison and a $3,000 fine.

### § 39–14–405. Aggravated Burglary.

a.   Aggravated burglary is burglary of a habitation as defined in Section 39-14-401.

b.   Aggravated burglary is a Class C felony punishable by up to 15 years in prison and a $5,000 fine.

### § 39–11–602. Criminal Responsibility for the Conduct of Another.

A person is criminally responsible for an offense committed by the conduct of another, if

a.   the person acts with intent to promote or assist the commission of the offense, or to benefit in the proceeds or results of the offense, and

b.   the person solicits, directs, aids, or attempts to aid another person to commit the offense.

## § 39–11–603. Criminal Responsibility for the Facilitation of Felony.

a.   A person is criminally responsible for the facilitation of a felony, if, knowing that another intends to commit a specific felony, but without the intent required for criminal responsibility under §39-11-402, the person knowingly furnishes substantial assistance in the commission of the felony.

b.   The facilitation of the commission of a felony is an offense of the class next below the felony facilitated by the person so charged.

## § 39–11–604. Accessory After the Fact.

a.   A person is an accessory after the fact who, after the commission of a felony, with knowledge or reasonable ground to believe that the offender has committed the felony, and with the intent to hinder the arrest, trial, conviction or punishment of the offender:

1.   Harbors or conceals the offender;

2.   Provides or aids in providing the offender with any means of avoiding arrest, trial, conviction or punishment; or

b.   This section shall have no application to an attorney providing legal services as required or authorized by law.

c.   Accessory after the fact is a Class A misdemeanor punishable by up to one year in prison and a $1,000 fine.

## ❱ Case Summaries from Law Clerk

Your law clerk, a law student from your alma mater, has been really impressive this semester. The clerk provides you with the following case summaries on the charged crimes and also suggests that you take a look at the elements of accessory after the fact as well:

**Relating to § 39–11–602. Criminal Responsibility for the Conduct of Another.**

*State v. Reyes* (2003): The culpable mental state of an aider and abettor is "intentional," as defined in § 39-11-602; thus, where evidence proved that the defendant was extremely intoxicated at the time that he handed the keys to his car over to his intoxicated girlfriend, defendant did not act intentionally when permitting her to operate his motor vehicle. Defendant did not have the requisite intent to be found criminally responsible for the crimes committed by the driver. Under § 39-11-602, proof of negligence or recklessness does not suffice to make a person criminally liable; it is necessary that defendant intend in some way associate himself with the venture, act with knowledge that an offense is to be committed, and share in the criminal intent of the principal.

*State v. Hundley* (1992): Conviction of wife under § 39-11-602 was proper because a person's participation in the crime may be inferred by evidence of presence and companionship with the perpetrator of a felony, in this case, the defendant's husband, before and after the commission of the offense. But mere presence during the commission of the crime is not enough to convict. The defendant was in the room where her husband made the counterfeit credit cards and identification cards, purchased goods with him at Target using the cards, and was by his side when he tried to use the ID to withdraw money from the bank.

*State v. Gooden* (1986): Even though the defendant did not enter the residence where the burglary occurred, the defendant was properly guilty of criminal responsibility for the act of another because the evidence proved that the defendant participated in the burglary by driving his friend to the home of the victim, parking at the corner and acting as a lookout, and then picking up his friend after the burglary.

**Cases relating to § 39–11–603. Criminal Responsibility for the Facilitation of Felony.**

*State v. Seaver* (1977): Facilitation is a lesser-included offense when the defendant is charged with criminal responsibility for the conduct of another. Where a person participates substantially in a felony but lacks the intent to promote, assist, or benefit from the offense, the trial court could have instructed the jury on the lesser-included offense of facilitation under § 39–11–603. In this case, the evidence showed that the defendant beat the victim with a baseball bat, but took no property from the victim. The jury could reasonably conclude that the defendant participated substantially in the robbery given the beating, but that the defendant did not intend to assist in or benefit from the co-defendant's removal of the victim's wallet.

*State v. Carter* (1988): The trial court properly charged the jury with the lesser-included offense of facilitation of possession of marijuana with the intent to sell when the baggies of marijuana were found in a jar in the defendant's backpack. The defendant admitted to putting the backpack in the trunk of the co-defendant's car. The co-defendant was also a known drug dealer, and the car smelled like someone had recently smoked marijuana.

**Cases relating to § 39–11–604. Accessory After the Fact.**

*State v. Wright* (2012): Evidence showed that the principal in
the murder told the defendant that he killed the victim, and the
defendant washed his bloodstained clothes and allowed him to
bury a knife in a box in her backyard. These actions amounted
to concealing and destroying evidence after the crime was
committed making her an accessory after the fact.

▶ **Exercise**

You will be assigned as either the prosecution or defense counsel
in this case. The above documents are available to both sides. Your
professor may also provide you with documents only available to your
side. Consider them carefully and remember that the opposing counsel will only learn about their contents if you choose to tell them.

There is no dispute here about whether the state has sufficient
evidence to prove beyond a reasonable doubt that Young and Smith
committed aggravated burglary. The negotiation is therefore limited
to whether or not both sides can agree to what, if anything, Calvin is
guilty of. Will there be a plea deal or will you go to trial? If you agree
to a plea, what is the appropriate punishment? If you cannot agree on
a plea, you will go forward with the preliminary hearing, and provided
that the prosecution shows that probable cause existed to arrest
Calvin, which is likely, the trial judge will set the case for trial.

Points to Consider

1. **The Criminal Statutes and Caselaw.** What crime or crimes, if any, is Calvin guilty of? (a) Look at the material elements in each statute covering various degrees of accomplice liability and determine whether Calvin's actions meet those elements. (b) Remember to use the case summaries to help you understand the elements of each crime. (c) Decide how you will use the law and cases in your negotiation.

2. **Accessory After the Fact.** Although this crime is not charged, either side can introduce another statute in a plea negotiation to see if the charges can be reduced or to argue that the facts map onto a different crime. Do you think Calvin was an accessory after the fact given the statute and case summary? What facts would and would not support charging this crime?

3. **The Facts.** The facts of the case help you evaluate whether the elements of each criminal charge could be established. What facts help your arguments most? What/Who are the sources of the facts in this case? Are the sources reliable? How can the presence of reliable or unreliable facts influence a plea negotiation?

4. **Intoxication.** Was Calvin intoxicated at the time of the aggravated burglary? What facts suggest that he was intoxicated / what facts hurt this argument? Does it matter whether he was intoxicated at the time?

5. **Collateral Consequences of a Conviction.** A conviction can result in a range of civil *collateral consequences* that can be harsher than even the criminal sentence. Here are some examples that apply to Calvin's life:

- *Voting*—If Calvin pleads to a felony, he loses the right to vote and other political rights.

- *Housing*—To save money, Calvin lives with his parents. Because Calvin's parents live in public housing, the housing authority will be notified of his arrest. If Calvin pleads to a misdemeanor that could be grounds to remove Calvin from his parent's lease or evict the family.

- *Employment*—Jobs, which are shown to reduce recidivism rates, may be harder to secure. Calvin was fired the next day from his job at Dick's Sporting Goods because he was incarcerated on Sunday and didn't show up for work. Long term, he also has to answer the following job application questions, which can hurt his chances to get a job: "Have you ever been arrested?" "Have you pleaded guilty to an offense?"

- *State Licensing*—A conviction could serve as a basis to deny Calvin a state license like a barber's license, a real estate license, or a medical license.

- *Immigration*—A conviction could be the basis for deportation.

Should collateral consequences factor into a plea negotiation? How can they factor in? Who should raise them?

6. **Negotiation Style.** Carefully consider the negotiation style that you plan to use with the opposing counsel. Are you more collaborative or competitive? How can that impact the negotiation? Does

it matter that both the prosecutor and defense counsel regularly deal with each other on other cases?

7. **Negotiation Strategy.**

   a.   The First Offer. Being the first to offer a resolution to the case can influence the entire negotiation and pull the other side closer to your position—This is known as an anchoring effect. Should you make the first offer? If not, how can you resist being anchored by the opposing side's offer?

   b.   Information Gathering. Questions can play a key role during a negotiation because they can help you learn more about the case, and more specifically about the other side's strategy and evidence. So don't be shy. Generate a list of questions for opposing counsel.

   c.   Silence and nonresponsive answers. Both can be important negotiation tools. Is there anything you don't want to reveal?

   d.   Exclusive information. What information do you have that you think the other side does not? Can it help you to reveal it?

## Negotiation Plan

### State v. Jones

1. Define Your Position

    a.   Offense Statutes—
What statutes, if any, do you think Calvin may be guilty of?
What is your best position?

    b.   Sentencing Range—
Consider the appropriate sentence for any statutes that you
would take a plea to.

    c.   Analysis of Facts—
How can the facts help you argue for different levels of culpability and sentencing ranges. Are there mitigating factors?

2. Establish Your Walk-Away Point
What is the worst position you will accept before you decide to
just go to trial and let a jury decide.

3. Opposing Counsel's Position
Try to predict your opposing counsel's initial position and walk
away point. Is there any overlap between the positions?

4. Negotiation Style and Strategy
Describe your intended negotiation style and strategy here.

## Plea Negotiation Outline